C000182892

Only God Will Save Us

Only God Will Save Us

The Nature of God and the Christian Life

Simon Cuff

scm press

© Simon Cuff 2020

Published in 2020 by SCM Press
Editorial office
3rd Floor, Invicta House,
108–114 Golden Lane,
London EC1Y 0TG, UK

www.scmpress.co.uk

SCM Press is an imprint of Hymns Ancient & Modern Ltd
(a registered charity)

Hymns Ancient & Modern® is a registered trademark of
Hymns Ancient & Modern Ltd
13A Hellesdon Park Road, Norwich,
Norfolk NR6 5DR, UK

British Library Cataloguing in Publication data
A catalogue record for this book is available
from the British Library

978-0-334-05926-4

Typeset by Regent Typesetting
Printed and bound by
CPI Group (UK) Ltd

Contents

Concepts create idols of God, of whom only wonder can tell us anything.
Attributed to St Gregory of Nyssa (c. 330–c. 390 CE)

Every concept which comes from some comprehensible image by an approximate understanding and by guessing at the divine nature constitutes an idol of God and does not proclaim God.
St Gregory of Nyssa[1]

1 Gregory of Nyssa, *Life of Moses*, trans. Malherbe, A. and Ferguson, E. (New York: Paulist Press, 1978), pp. 95–6.

For those who reveal the God of life.

Acknowledgements

I owe a debt of thanks to all at SCM Press, and especially David Shervington for his continued guidance and support. Thanks are also due to the staff of the British Library on whose work this book relies. My family, especially my nephews and nieces, remain a source of inspiration and I continue to rely on the prayers of my cell group, Carol, John, and Di. The content of this book has been more than a decade in the writing, and particular thanks go to Philip Kennedy, Mark Knight, Jane Williams, Fr Peter Groves, Mthr Jenn Strawbridge, Fr Lincoln Harvey, Fr Michael Leyden, Mthr Donna Lazenby, (Fr) Nick Griffin, Jared Lovell, Selina Stone, Renie Choy, Fr Gregory Platten and many others who have encouraged me and revealed to me the beauty of the doctrine of God that this book attempts to articulate, however poorly. Thanks also to the people of St Cyprian's Clarence Gate, who welcomed and supported me so warmly and sustained me through this project, and special thanks go to Fr Michael Fuller for his encouragement at every turn. Fr Jonathan Jong is owed special thanks and bears particular responsibility for commissioning a series on the doctrine of God for St Mary Magdalen's School of Theology (www.theschooloftheology.org). Chapter 4 originally appeared as an article in the journal *Crucible*, and I'm thankful for Matt Bullimore's insightful comments on the text. I'm thankful too for the students of St Mellitus Northwest, clergy of Sheffield Diocese, and those exploring vocation in Chichester Diocese who each contributed to earlier versions of the lecture which gave rise to my reflections on the wrath of

God. I'm particularly thankful to Lucy Hodges for suggesting the work of the artist Anne Grebby for the cover image, and for Anne Grebby (www.annegrebby.com) for kindly giving permission for her work 'man ascending and descending' to be used for the cover. Once again, this book would have been impossible without the support of Fr Jack Noble. All mistakes remain my own.

Introduction:
The God of Classical Theism

> Theology has at its heart only one problem: God. God is the passion of theologians, their torment and their delight. But God can only be loved 'with all our heart and with all our soul and with all our might'. So a theologian must be wholly concentrated. We cannot do theology half-heartedly, or with a divided mind or soul, or merely by the way. Theologians will bring the whole of their existence into their search for knowledge about God. (Jürgen Moltmann)[1]

Theology sometimes gets a bad press. It's written off as something overly dry or abstract produced by stale clergy or academics. There *is* a lot of dry and abstract theology, but theology that is overly dry or abstract is often *bad* theology.

Theology is the task of speaking about God. If the theology we produce is dry or abstract we're probably not doing a very good job at speaking about the living God, the God of Abraham, Isaac and Jacob, who is anything but dry or abstract.

All theology is to an extent bad theology. The best theology produced by the best theological minds will be as nothing compared to the glory of seeing the living God face to face. However, there is theology that is very bad at articulating God, and there is theology that is less bad. The task of theology is to find the best available ways of thinking and speaking about God.

Some ways of thinking and being fall much further short than others in articulating the God we worship. Such ways are often referred to as heresy, which in some respects is the counterpoint to Christian orthodoxy. The term 'heresy' comes from the Greek *hairesis,* meaning 'choice'. It is then applied to particular opinions or schools of thought, as we find the term in the book of Acts: 'the sect (*heresy*) of the Sadducees' (Acts 5.17), and 'the sect (*heresy*) of the Pharisees' (Acts 15.5). Eventually the term becomes a technical one for those who differ from orthodox Christian teaching. We can see the term begin to be used in this way with the New Testament: 'false teachers among you, who will secretly bring in destructive opinions (*heresies*)' (2 Peter 2.1).

Heresy is contrasted to orthodoxy, meaning 'right belief'. Christian orthodoxy has developed over centuries in the promulgation of creeds and in the discernment of the canon of Scripture. What are now considered heresies were often important stepping stones in the discovery of orthodoxy.[2] This or that heresy forced the Church to articulate clearly an orthodox position to explain the inferiority of these heretical views. For example, the heresy of Arianism stemmed from the Alexandrian presbyter Arius in the fourth century, who considered the Son a creature and only the Father as God without beginning or act of creation. Combatting Arianism forced the Church to articulate clearly the divinity of the Son, affirmed as the Second Person of the Trinity and therefore not part of the created order.

There are many other enticing delights in the basket of heresies available to those who would try to follow Christ. There are rarely new forms of heretical thinking. Instead, the same ideas emerge again and again as Christians wrestle with the task of attempting to speak well or less badly about the God we worship. All heresies have at least one thing in common. They're a simple, and usually attractive, means of making some aspect of the Christian faith easier to understand than what is maintained within Christian orthodoxy. They often seek to smooth or iron out frustrating tensions that Christian orthodoxy seems quite happy to let stand.

Heresies also almost always have unintended consequences. They often seem to be the more obvious option when viewing a particular doctrine or belief in isolation. They make an aspect of the faith easier to swallow, but can cause problems further down the theological line. For example, the heresy of Apollinarianism (from the teaching of Apollinarius c. 310–90 CE) teaches that Jesus had a fully human body but the human mind of Jesus was replaced by God in the Incarnation. It's perhaps easier for us to understand how God replaced the human mind of Christ in the Incarnation, rather than to worry ourselves about how a fully human mind and body had space to fit God in too.[3]

The problems that heresies give rise to further down the theological line are often in the area of soteriology (how God saves us in Christ) and Christology (who we say Christ is). These two branches of theology are the litmus test of any theological offering. Heretical views are often heretical precisely because they render us unable to give an account of the saving work of God in Christ, or they force us to give an account that does not adequately describe what has been revealed to us by God through Christ. Apollinarianism fails as a description of Christ because it leaves untouched an aspect of ourselves that needs redemption, as theologians at the time realized. Christ must have had a human mind if the whole of our humanity is to be redeemed.

One of the best ways to make sure our theology is articulating the God we worship is to ensure that it is this God who is always solidly in view. As human beings, we have an awful knack of being able to make *ourselves* the focus of our theology, whether we mean to or not. We find ways of elevating some human ways of thinking or speaking about God that we happen to like, and we worship them as if they were God himself. We almost always don't realize that this is what we are doing, and we cling to that way of thinking or speaking, fearing that God might let go of us if we let go of our own favourite way of thinking or speaking about him.

This book is unashamedly theological. It seeks to keep the nature of God squarely in view as we think about what it means for us to live and act in a world in which we do not yet see God face to face. Theology begins a process of thinking and speaking about God, but it does not end there. 'In the beginning was the Word, and the Word was with God, and the Word was God' we read in John's prologue (John 1.1), but this is not the end of the matter. In fact, we know it's only the beginning. 'The Word becomes flesh' (John 1.14). A theology that is limited only to ways of thinking and speaking about God is also likely to be bad theology. Good theology is not limited to speaking about God, but motivates us to offer the whole of ourselves in worship and service of the living God who is the ground and centre of all *theo*-logy. If theology has the living God in view, it changes the way we live and act in the world. Or it should.

This book seeks to ask: What does Christian life and action look like if we are in the business of thinking theologically? What consequences for how we act flow from the nature of the God we worship? What does it mean for the Christian life if God is truly the centre of our thinking and being?

The God of Classical Theism

There is an observable trend in the course of the theology of the twentieth century to transform our speaking and teaching about God in the light of legitimate human experience and self-understanding. This book takes the contrary approach – asking how human action can be transformed in the light of a classic theological understanding of God. This is not to belittle the salient strengths of modern theology in overcoming some weaknesses in the classical doctrine, particularly in the perceived distance of God from the everyday realities of human-kind. Instead, we shall see how a renewed focus on the classic theological understanding of God equips us as human beings to confront many of the evils that lie behind the tendency of modern theologies to advocate a God in our image.

This book therefore seeks to draw on the tradition of thinking and speaking about God that has become known as classical theism. This is the fruit of centuries of reflection on the nature and revelation of God. Classical theism is a significant attempt to make the ways we think and speak about God be in line with his nature as revealed to us in Scripture.

Classical theism describes God's nature in terms of certain attributes. In technical terms it teaches that God is omnipotent, omniscient, omnibenevolent, immutable, impassible and simple. Put in less technical language, God is all-powerful, all-knowing, all-good, unchanging, incapable of suffering, and not made up of bits or parts. When put in these terms, the God of 'classical theism' doesn't seem so alien from the God we sing about in our hymns and worship songs.

The attributes of classical theism are probably most familiar to students beginning to study theology through the problem of evil: how is it that a God who is all-powerful, all-knowing and all-good allows suffering? We will not attempt to provide a solution to the problem of evil here. However, we will touch upon suffering in Chapter 2 as we explore how the God who cannot suffer suffers in Christ or, more technically, as we discover how the impassible God takes on passibility in Christ.

Throughout Christian history the suffering of Christ has generated fierce discussion when viewed alongside the attributes of God according to classical theism. If Jesus is God, as the Church believes, how is it that a God who is incapable of suffering can be said to suffer for our sakes by death on a cross? Some Christians have wanted, for this and other commendable reasons, to say that God does in fact suffer. Traditionally the Church has insisted that only a God incapable of suffering can save us. We will explore how it is that God relates to suffering in Christ, and what this means for how we live and act in a world of suffering.

In fact, it is not only God's inability to suffer that has been questioned in the course of Christian thinking over the last century. Every single one of these attributes has been hotly debated. For example, what does it mean for God to be all-powerful? Can he do anything and everything? Or is he just able to do anything that is logically possible to do? Philosophically minded theologians have enjoyed (possibly too much) asking themselves whether God is able to make a stone that he finds impossible to lift. Such mental gymnastics are not the concern of this book. Indeed, they can often be off-putting and seem at first to have little to do with the God of Abraham, Isaac and Jacob, the God we worship.

It is sometimes thought that the God of classical theism is a product of the kind of dry and abstract thinking we noted above, which often produces bad theology. This 'god of the philosophers' is said to have little to do with the God we worship. The philosopher Blaise Pascal famously had an experience of God which made him regard the god of philosophy as distinct from the God of the Bible. He wrote in his journal on 23 November 1654, 'Fire. The God of Abraham, the God of Isaac, the God of Jacob, and not of philosophers and men of science.'[4] More recently, the liberation theologian Gustavo Gutiérrez has repeated this view: 'The God of the Bible is not the God of philosophy. This is an authentically Christian insight that has legitimately inspired many lived experiences and reflections. It is impossible not to agree with it.'[5]

The God of non-Christian philosophical speculation is not the God of the Bible. The God of classical theism is not the God of philosophy. Each of the attributes of the God of classical theism finds its basis in Scripture. For example, God's omnipotence, or ability to do anything, is described in St Luke's Gospel, 'for nothing will be impossible for God' (Luke 1.37). Likewise, God's immutability or inability to change can be found in the letter of St James, where God is described as 'the Father of lights, with whom there is no variation or shadow due to change' (James 1.17). The God of classical theism *is* the God of the Bible.

However, the assertion is often made that the God of classical theism is a philosophical intrusion into the biblical witness. More often than not this is offered as a critically unexamined trope. As we shall see throughout what follows, the classical attributes of God reflect the nature of the God we find in Scripture and subsequent Christian orthodoxy.

Criticisms of classical theism increased across the twentieth century. Various theologians attempted to do away with one or other of the classical attributes, often for what seem like very good reasons. In particular, the impassability of God came under attack. It was felt necessary for God to suffer in order to enter into solidarity with human beings who suffer.

However, to do away with the classical attributes so easily might have unintended consequences. Undermining God's inability to suffer impacts upon God's ability to transform the very suffering that gave rise to the desire for him to enter into suffering solidarity in the first place. For the Dominican theologian Herbert McCabe, it represents a kind of idolatry: 'The idea of God suffering in sympathy with creation represents a regrettable regression from the traditional insistence on the mystery of God and can be seen as a kind of idolatry.'[6]

Idolatry is a constant theme of this book. All too often, the temptation to do away with one or other of these classical attributes stems from making an aspect of human thinking or experience primary, and interpreting our doctrine of God in its light. Rather than focusing on the nature of God, and asking how God transforms human ways of thinking and being, some of these theologians have sought instead to re-describe the nature of God. All too easily this means that humanity becomes the focus of this theology rather than the nature of God himself. This is at the root of all forms of idolatry.

Idolatry is the elevation of something human or created so that it becomes an object of worship, which should be reserved solely for God. In cases of idolatry, God is re-made in our image, rather than us in his. God is made to be like us.

Jane Williams notes the shock that we might feel at realizing that the incarnation is not about God becoming like us, but rather about human beings becoming like him: 'Sad, egocentric, embittered, and self-obsessed as we are, we have tended to assume that Jesus became human like us, but now, illuminatingly, we discover that we are invited to become human like him.'[7]

This book does not set out to provide an exhaustive defence of the God of classical theism. Rather than seeking to re-describe God in the light of human experience, this book seeks to ask how the reality of human experience might be transformed by the nature of God himself. Above all, this book is about action. What does it mean to act in such a way that the nature of God is kept squarely in view at all times? What does Christian action look like that keeps idolatry to a minimum, inescapable as it is given the human tendency to make idols?

Opponents of classical theism may rightly, and fruitfully, argue against this or that attribute of God. Such work is important in making sure that the theology of God within classical theism does not itself become an idol. For the sake of exploring the fruits of such a doctrine of God, however, we assume the God of classical theism. The fruits of such a doctrine might themselves tell in favour of the concept of God as classically understood.

The Living God

This book assumes the God of classical theism in order to explore what Christian action looks like when it flows from this doctrine. While differing from Gutiérrez's suspicion of the God of classical theism, this book develops an insight found elsewhere in his work.

Gutiérrez notes that God's nature is not shaped by his action in the world. What God does in relation to the world does not shape how God is in himself. Rather, God's being is the source of his action:

God is not a liberator because God liberates; rather God liberates because God is a liberator. God is not just because God establishes justice, or faithful because God enters into a covenant, but the other way round. I am not playing with words here, but trying to bring out the primacy and transcendence of God and to remind ourselves that God's being gives meaning to God's action.[8]

Instead of trying to make God like us, what would our lives look like if we tried to make our action correspond ever more closely with his? We know that to act completely like God is impossible. It transcends our creaturely limits and we also lack the capacity to be morally perfect because of the limitations of our humanity. We sin and, as the life, death and resurrection of Jesus remind us, we are always in need of redemption.

However, we know too that God invites us to reflect on our ways of being and acting in the world. The proclamation of the Gospel and the living of the Christian life is an invitation to be constantly open to being transformed and conformed more closely to that image of God in which all of us are created. This book seeks to reflect on the nature of God, and God's action in relation to creation, as a means of reflecting on our own action and living out of the Christian life. In doing so, we must avoid the inevitable temptation to make ourselves and *our* action the focus of our life and thought. Instead we are trying to focus always on God in order that our action might flow from that focus.

God is primary here. There are other well-known theological formulations of this idea. Karl Rahner famously noted that who God is, is what God does. He related this insight to the Trinity, using technical language to describe how what God does is how God is: 'the "economic" Trinity is the "immanent" Trinity and the "immanent" Trinity is the "economic" Trinity'.[9] The action of God that gives rise to our experience of him is identical with how God is in himself. Put simply, God simply is.

In the book of Exodus, when Moses asks for God's name,

God responds: 'I am who I am' (Exod. 3.14). As John Durham notes in his commentary, the verb 'to be' here connotes

> continuing, unfinished action: 'I am being that I am being,' or 'I am the Is-ing One,' that is, 'the One Who Always Is.' Not conceptual being, being in the abstract, but active being ... It is a reply that suggests that it is inappropriate to refer to God as 'was' or as 'will be,' for the reality of active existence can be suggested only by the present: 'is' or 'is-ing,' 'Always Is', or 'Am'.[10]

The eternal 'is-ness' of God will be the subject of our first chapter. Divine simplicity is the notion that God is God, that God is foundational in Godself and he is not a being of composite parts. We will introduce the concept of divine simplicity in some detail because of its importance in establishing the doctrine of God according to classical theism.

Nicholas Wolterstorff notes the fecundity of this doctrine in classical theology:

> If one grants God's simplicity, then one also has to grant a large number of other divine attributes: immateriality, eternity, immutability ... If one grants that God is simple, one's interpretation of all God's other attributes will have to be formed in the light of that conviction.[11]

We will argue that divine simplicity is simply a reminder that God is God, and not just another agent within creation. However, it is also important to discuss divine simplicity because it is one of the most hotly contested attributes of the God of classical theism. Many Christians struggle to understand how anything can be truly simple, not made up of any aspects or parts. They instead prefer to do away with divine simplicity or complexify simplicity with a number of qualifications.

For the overall argument of this book, focusing on divine simplicity will prove to be important because it enables us to hold together both God's nature and his action, and also each of the attributes of God that appear to us at first glance to be contradictory. A strong understanding of divine simplicity encourages us to think of the mercy of God as we think of the justice of God as we think of the love of God and so on. This in turn encourages us to reflect on the unity of our action. It encourages us to integrate the various aspects of our compartmentalized selves, to focus more clearly on God in all that we do, and to allow all that we do to flow from a focus on God in the heart of our lives.

Gutiérrez's insight is therefore especially important for our task. He reminds us that God's nature informs his action. This might strike us as obvious. It is another way of saying that God cannot do anything that is out of character. God simply is. His action is always in accordance with his being. We are also reminded that the same is not true for us. While our actions are shaped by the kind of people we are, we are able to do things that are not in keeping with our character. The kindest of us can sometimes be mean. The angriest of us can sometimes be gentle. Even the most evil can sometimes perform some kind of good deed.

Our character shapes the kind of actions we perform, but it does not completely determine them. Our character is itself shaped by the kind of actions we perform. We become kind through practising deeds of kindness. We become known as a kind person by others because we have done several acts of kindness.

The same is not true for God. God acts because God is. This book asks what our actions might look like if we based them on the way God is in himself. What might our action in the world look like if we tried to act in accordance with the nature of God? What might our action look like if we tried to make our action in the world conform to his action in and towards the world? To use Gutiérrez's examples, if we liberate because God is a liberator, if we seek justice because God is just, if we act faithfully because God is faithful? What might our action look like if we made God's nature primary in our action, if we put God front and centre not only of our thinking and speaking about him, but in everything we do?

God for the Church

Wolterstorff reminded us of the theoretical fecundity of divine simplicity for the theologians of classical theism. We shall argue that classical theism offers not only theoretical fecundity for thinking about God but practical fecundity in the living of the Christian life and the proclamation of the Gospel.

Such practical fecundity is sorely needed in the Church. What Martin Luther King wrote in 1963 might well be written about the Church of today:

> the contemporary church is often a weak, ineffectual voice with an uncertain sound. It is so often the arch-supporter of the status quo. Far from being disturbed by the presence of the church, the power structure of the average community is consoled by the church's silent and often vocal sanction of things as they are. But the judgement of God is upon the church as never before. If the church of today does not recapture the sacrificial spirit of the early church, it will lose its authentic ring, forfeit the loyalty of millions, and be dismissed.[12]

Contemporary doctrines of God often unwittingly become servants of the status quo, which King reminds us ought always to be disturbed by God's transforming presence through his Church. At worst, contemporary doctrines of God postulate a God who can be as much transformed by the status quo as he transforms it, who grieves at the injustice of the status quo but cannot transcend it, who changes in relation to the status quo but is limited in his ability to change it. All too often in the face of the injustice of the status quo, contemporary doctrines of God unwittingly invoke a God who relates to such injustice as *we* do, rather than a God who transcends and transforms such injustice.

The God of classical theism is sorely needed to overcome the status quo and to help the Church to resist the ever-present temptation to be the 'silent and often vocal sanction of things as they are'. The God of classical theism is the God who is not transformed by the injustice of the way the world is ordered, but transforms it. The God of classical theism is the God who confronted death on the cross and defeated it. Crucially, the God of classical theism is not us. Classical theism invites us to let God be God. It illuminates our creaturely limitations and brings to our attention where the ever-present temptation to put ourselves at the centre of things is both distorting our view of God and also encouraging us to support the injustice of the status quo.

As human beings, we are for ever making god in our image and putting ourselves at centre stage. In the history of Christian action in the world, all too often Christians have usurped the place of God by celebrating our own power and agency. Modern theology has seen the very concept of God recast to more closely resemble human ways of being. Notions of God have been transformed in the light of the extent of the suffering and injustice experienced in the twentieth century, while many of the mechanisms within human society that contributed to such suffering remain as quietly sanctioned status quo. In the face of the suffering which has given rise to such transformation in the doctrine of God within modern theology, it is we who need to be transformed. It is we who need to be laid on the cross of contemporary theology. We need to be transformed by God, not him by us.

Joerg Rieger notes that such transformation has widespread consequences for the life of the Church. He notes that even in our mission and evangelism we have usurped God's role and made ourselves the focus by celebrating 'our ability to transform others and make them more Christian'.[13] He asks: 'what if the most important thing in mission ... is not what we are doing but what God is doing?'[14] This focus is at the heart of this book: shaping what *we* are doing by focusing on who God *is*: what he does and is doing.

However, Rieger also reminds us that caution is needed here too: 'God can be claimed for almost anything'.[15] Rieger's notion of mission puts God first in order to try and prevent us claiming God for ourselves. Reflection on the nature of God is crucial to this process of putting God first. By focusing on our doctrine of God, we lessen the risk of unwittingly creating idols for ourselves or putting ourselves front and centre even in our doctrine of God.

To put God first, to focus on what God is doing, Rieger suggests, requires us

> to give up control, to commit things to God ... This latter part is, of course, the most difficult one. But here it shows whether we truly trust in God's grace. The biggest challenge, however, is that this reversal forces us to take a deeper look at ourselves. Before we can become part of the solution, we need to develop a self-critical attitude that helps us reflect on how we have come to be (and still are) part of the problem.[16]

What follows is the first stage in such a self-critical exploration. Our exploration of the God of classical theism reminds us that instead of making God in our image, we are always invited to be remade into his. An initial chapter introduces the concept of divine simplicity (that God is fully God without being made up of bits or parts or attributes of himself). We then explore some of the attributes of God in this light, what it means for God to suffer, to love, to be angry, to show mercy, and to be jealous. Finally two more practical chapters explore what such an understanding of God means for our prayer lives and for how we might live the Christian life in the light of doctrine of God.

The focus of this book is the doctrine of God, which can initially seem heavy going. However, as we shall see, this is a crucial stage in developing a responsible account of Christian action. It is vital for Christians who wish to act in accordance with the will of God, and in line with the image in which they are created, to know that it is truly God who is at the centre of all that they do.

Each chapter is designed to begin with a brief exploration of the doctrine of God before exploring the consequences of that aspect of the doctrine for the Christian life. As individual chapters progress, and as the book as a whole unfolds, our exploration focuses more and more on the practical task of living the Christian life in the light of the doctrine of God.

Throughout what follows we consider the classical doctrine of God, what sort of Christian action might flow from this doctrine, and how therefore we might better contribute to what God is already doing through his Church to transform every unjust status quo.

Notes

1 Moltmann, J., *Experiences in Theology: Ways and Forms of Christian Theology* (London: SCM Press, 2000), p. 23.

2 See especially Edwards, M., *Catholicity and Heresy in the Early Church* (Farnham: Ashgate, 2009).

3 Christian orthodoxy rejects phrasing the question in such a way, affirming that God is both fully human and fully divine in a way that completes the human, but does not compete with the human in Christ. This observation is the central argument of Rowan Williams, *Christ the Heart of Creation* (London: Bloomsbury Continuum, 2018).

4 Pascal, B., *Pensées* (Baltimore: Penguin, 1966), p. 309 (cited in Ward, K., 'The God of the Philosophers and the God of Abraham, Isaac, and Jacob', in *The Journal of Jewish Thought and Philosophy* 8 (1999), pp. 157–70, 157).

5 Gutiérrez, G., 'Understanding the God of Life', in Nickoloff, J. (ed.), *Gustavo Gutiérrez: Essential Writings* (London: SCM Press, 1996), pp. 60–4, 61.

6 McCabe, H., *God Matters* (London: Continuum, 2010), p. 1.

7 Williams, J., 'O Rex Gentium: O King of the Nations', in *The Church Times* (21 December 2018), available at: www.churchtimes.

co.uk/articles/2018/21-december/faith/faith-features/o-rex-gentium-o-king-of-the-nations (accessed 29.3.19).

8 Gutiérrez, G., *The God of Life* (Maryknoll: Orbis Books, 1991), p. 2.

9 Rahner, K., *The Trinity*, trans. Donceel, J. (New York: Crossroad, 1997), p. 22.

10 Durham, J. I., *Word Biblical Commentary, Vol. 3, Exodus* (Waco, TX: Word Books, 1987), p. 39.

11 Wolterstorff, N., 'Divine Simplicity', in *Philosophical Perspectives, Vol. 5, Philosophy of Religion* (1991), pp. 531–52.

12 King, M. L., *Letter from Birmingham Jail* (Stanford: Overbrook Press, 1968), p. 14.

13 Rieger, J., 'Theology and Mission Between Neocolonialism and Postcolonialism', in *Mission Studies* 21.2 (2004), pp. 201–27, 219.

14 Rieger, 'Theology and Mission', p. 219.

15 Rieger, 'Theology and Mission', p. 219.

16 Rieger, 'Theology and Mission', p. 221.

I

Divine Simplicity

If they had known the Scriptures, and been taught by the truth, they would have known, beyond doubt, that God is not as men are; and that His thoughts are not like the thoughts of men. For the Father of all is at a vast distance from those affections and passions which operate among men. He is a simple, uncompounded Being, without diverse members, and altogether like, and equal to himself, since He is wholly understanding, and wholly spirit, and wholly thought, and wholly intelligence, and wholly reason, and wholly hearing, and wholly seeing, and wholly light, and the whole source of all that is good. (St Irenaeus of Lyons)[1]

Divine simplicity is a deceptively named concept. Far from simple, it's a concept which is difficult to understand. There is good reason for this. At its heart, divine simplicity reminds us that God is like nothing we encounter in creation. Whereas everything we encounter is 'composite' or made up of parts, God is not. God is simply God. There are no bits to him or aspects of himself that are prior to him. He is simply what or who he is.

Moreover, God is simple in terms of his attributes. He is identical with them. God doesn't just love or have love, he is love. As John Behr notes:

Likewise for all the other divine attributes, wisdom, truth, omnipotence, and so on; yet if each of these is not something that God 'has,' as distinct from himself, but they are each what God is, they must, as applied to God, be identical in meaning, describing the same reality, even if for us, as we conceive them, they are formally distinct.[2]

This prayer of St Anselm (1033–1109 CE) encapsulates this notion of divine simplicity:

> There are no parts in you, Lord; neither are you many, but you are so much one and the same with yourself that in nothing are you dissimilar with yourself. Indeed you are unity itself not divisible by any mind. Life and wisdom and the other (attributes), then, are not parts of you, but all are one and each of them is wholly what you are and what all the others are.[3]

We begin with divine simplicity because, as we noted in the introduction, divine simplicity has consequences for everything else we think and say about God. As Nicholas Wolterstorff has noted, if God is simple 'then one also has to grant a large number of other divine attributes: immateriality, eternity, immutability'.[4] If God is simple he cannot be made up of stuff because that would require him to be composite. If God is simple, he cannot be mutable (changeable) or subject to time because that would require him to go from one state to another, which would mean he was not simply God.

Such an understanding of God is fairly alien to much modern theological understanding. Our picture of God or the ways we think and speak about him often present him as a composite being. He is often presented as an agent who bears a striking resemblance to us. He might be better than us, more powerful than us, more faithful than us, but often he is a God in our own image. We often have an image of the 'God' we need to do that which we want to do – to 'fight our battles' – or we gravitate towards church traditions who display a way of thinking or speaking about God to which *we* can relate. This can be true even within academic theology, where the fundamental categories with which the success or failure of a doctrine of God is judged are human ones. The limitations of human comprehension become the test case of a good or bad doctrine of God, as we shall see below.

We turn now to focus on the doctrine of divine simplicity. We focus on this aspect of the nature of God at some length because it is perhaps the most alien of the classical attributes. Divine simplicity is also the ground upon which the rest of the argument of this book is set.

The doctrine of divine simplicity was once held in common by both Catholic and Protestant theology as a shared feature of the Christian doctrine of God. James Dolezal points out that 'the doctrine's ecumenical credentials are truly impressive. Historically it has been confessed by Orthodox churches, Roman Catholics, Anglicans, Presbyterians, Congregationalists, and Baptists ... But this common confession of divine simplicity is no longer common.'[5] Divine simplicity has been abandoned in much modern theological discourse, or as Thomas White notes, 'more commonly it has simply been ignored'.[6]

However, divine simplicity is making somewhat of a comeback, even if its recovery and re-articulation are still in an infant stage.[7] A wave of recent publications have sought to defend the simplicity of God according to classical theism.[8] Others defend a slightly altered form of the doctrine.[9] However, like the simple God the doctrine espouses, divine simplicity is difficult to alter without fundamentally disturbing the insight which it gives us into the nature of God.

Divine simplicity stems from two important features of the Christian doctrine of God. Firstly, Christian monotheism, the oneness or unity of God. Secondly, the fundamental distinction between God as creator and his creation. We will return to this distinction throughout this chapter and the book as a whole.

It is important to note that divine simplicity is, like all theology, as much a set of rules or grammar about how we can speak less badly of God as it is a substantive claim about God's nature. White notes that 'any notion of divine unity is predicated upon some account of divine simplicity. When we seek to say how the persons of the Trinity are one we inevitably must speak by comparative similitude with creatures.'[10]

White alerts us to the fact that divine simplicity results from an affirmation of the unity of God and his distinction from the created order:

> We cannot understand rightly what it means to say that God is one unless we clarify how the unity of God differs from or is like that of creatures. Unity occurs in creatures insofar as they are unified composites. In what way, then, is the one God like or unlike the composite creatures he has made? To ask this question is to ask the question of divine simplicity.[11]

At one level, divine simplicity is a reminder about what we *cannot* say about God. We cannot say that what it means for him to be one is what it means for us to be one. In that sense, divine simplicity stands in the tradition of 'apophatic' or negative theology which affirms truths about God by ruling out what God is not.[12]

Apophatic theology is often misunderstood as reducing our ability to speak about God. However, apophatic theology can provide us with a lot we can say about God. As we shall see below when we encounter Nicholas of Cusa's notion of God as 'not another', negative theology can open up as many ways of speaking well about God as it closes down ways in which we are likely to speak idolatrously or create a God in our own image.

Negative theology reminds us that much of what we say about God is analogical. We apply our creaturely experience to our descriptions of the creator by way of analogy or comparison. Negative theology reminds us that such speech is analogy and does not fully describe the mystery of God. White notes that

> we can speak absolutely truly of God in a mediated analogical fashion, based upon a careful series of negations of

compositions we find in creatures. And we can say many very important non-trivial things about what God is in himself, including the things we have said here about divine simplicity. But what we cannot do is know in a direct way what the simplicity of God is in itself.[13]

Such negative theology also enables us to recognize, in White's terms, 'the gratuity of supernatural revelation'.[14] Where we are able to speak positively of God through revelation, negative theology reminds us that such revelation is given to us as gift: 'God is truly sharing his own life with us, inviting us into something that completely transcends the ordinary range of our natural knowledge and its limited capacities.'[15]

The most common ground for a rejection of divine simplicity is a rejection of this ultimate distinction between creature and creation. James Dolezal notes the 'outstanding common denominator [in arguments against the doctrine of divine simplicity is that] ... each critic speaks as if God and creatures were "beings" in the exact same sense, reducing the Creator-creature distinction'.[16] Dolezal notes that divine simplicity is a consequence of affirming the distinction between creature and Creator. To deny divine simplicity, he suggests, means 'that God is regarded as merely another being within the world, even if the most supreme instance of such being'.[17] White agrees: 'emphasis on the divine simplicity elicits increased awareness of the transcendence of God with respect to his creation'.[18]

As we shall see, the distinction between creature and Creator is fundamental to the classical theist affirmation of divine simplicity. Modern critics who downplay such a distinction by including God and creation within the same account of what is (in technical terms 'ontology') in effect describe a God who is fundamentally similar to us. When the distinction between creature and Creator is not affirmed clearly, divine simplicity makes little sense. We end up in the situation described by Wolterstoff: 'not only can we not devise an acceptable account of divine simplicity; we cannot even understand accounts presented to us by the medievals which they found non-problematic'.[19]

Divine simplicity is therefore grounded in the confession of God as Creator. Keith Ward puts this confession succinctly when he notes that the Christian doctrine of creation 'is not the doctrine that this universe began in time. It is the doctrine that every time is absolutely dependent for its existence on a timeless reality that stands beyond it and yet is its ontological foundation.'[20] God holds all of creation in being 'in one single, timeless, creative act of origination'.[21] Affirming divine simplicity is a consequence of acknowledging that until the Incarnation God is 'outside' the world of created beings he is calling into existence and to which he relates. Whereas we and all creatures, even time itself, rely on him for our existence, God stands outside the world of composites as pure existence. He simply is.

The Doctrine of Creation as Foundation for Divine Simplicity

It is often stated that divine simplicity is unscriptural because we encounter a God on the pages of Scripture who does not seem to be simple in the way divine simplicity suggests. Brian Davies discusses the views of those who insist that there is 'an enormous gulf between the God of classical theism and the God of the Bible since the former is static and remote while the latter is dynamic and involved ... [which] seems to me an awful misreading of classical theism'.[22] The God of classical theism that we will spell out on these pages demonstrates a God who is anything but static. The Incarnation, a central feature of the Christian account of the God of classical theism, is the ultimate disproof that the God of classical theism is static or inert. The God of classical theism is the Creator who transforms his creation from the inside in the Incarnation, becoming one of us in Christ.

Moreover, it is important to note that one of earliest witnesses to divine simplicity in the Christian tradition, St Irenaeus of Lyons (c.130–c.200 CE), asserts divine simplicity against his opponents with the introduction 'if they had known the Scriptures'.[23] His opponents were a group of heretics known in scholarship as 'gnostics', who taught that God is made up of a series of processions and emanations (or parts) and is therefore composite.[24] The Christian concept of God, meanwhile, is simple: 'He is a simple, uncompounded Being, without diverse members, and altogether like, and equal to himself.'[25]

For our purposes it is important to notice that Irenaeus does not derive divine simplicity from a pagan or philosophical source. While he notes that even 'the religious and pious are wont to speak concerning God',[26] and he can describe divine simplicity using pagan philosophical resources,[27] his *source* is Christian Scripture. He alludes to Isaiah 55.8 ('My thoughts are not your thoughts, nor are your ways my ways, says the Lord') to make the fundamental distinction between God and his creatures: 'God is not as men are.'[28]

Divine simplicity for Irenaeus is revealed in the Christian doctrine of creation and the distinction between creation and 'the Father of all creatures' that we have begun to trace. Elsewhere in *Against Heresies* Irenaeus makes this distinction clear: 'in this respect God differs from man, that God indeed makes, but man is made; and truly, He who makes is always the same; but that which is made must receive both beginning, and middle, and addition, and increase'.[29] After stating this distinction between creature and Creator, Irenaeus once again grounds it in the doctrine of divine simplicity: 'God also is truly perfect in all things, Himself equal and similar to Himself.'[30]

Likewise the distinction between creature and Creator is key to understanding another important account of divine simplicity, that of St Thomas Aquinas (1225–74) in his *Summa Theologica*.[31] Aquinas devotes an article (I.3) to the question of God's simplicity. As Rowan Williams observes, often within Christian theology 'later puzzles and apparent dead ends in doctrinal reflection can be transformed by a better understanding of what we discover that Aquinas has already discussed'.[32] Divine simplicity is no exception.

Aquinas begins his discussion of divine simplicity by asking whether God is a body or composed of matter and form (I.3.1–2). He rejects these on the grounds that God is pure act. By saying that God is 'pure act' he means that there is no potential in God – he simply is. Put another way, there is no other way of being God or else God would not be perfectly God. There can be no other way of being God: he simply is who he is. There follow some technical discussions, including whether God is identical to what it means to be God (I.3.3) and whether what it means to be God and what it means for God to 'exist' are the same (I.3.4), before turning directly to the question of God's simplicity.[33]

Aquinas answers that God is simply God, unlike a human being who is a particular instance of humanity: 'humanity and a man are not wholly identical ... since God then is not composed of matter and form, He must be His own Godhead, His own Life, and whatever else is thus predicated of Him'.[34]

Throughout this article, Aquinas appeals to God's role as Creator as the grounds for divine simplicity. Composite creation requires a cause or creator, whereas no such external cause can be presupposed of God. As uncaused, there is nothing prior or external to him. If there were to be something prior or external to him, then he would not be the creator of it. Therefore, he must be simple.

This distinction between creation and Creator is central to Rowan Williams' *Christ the Heart of Creation*. A key theme in his argument concerns the 'non-competitive relation of Creator and creation ... clarity about this can play a vital role in clarifying certain themes in ethics and politics for the Christian'.[35] This insight is part of the inspiration for this present book. Williams hints at conclusions for Christian action on the theme of competition from reflection on the distinctiveness of God in relation to creation. Since God's action in the world is not competitive with ours, certain ethics of competition and domination are ruled out. Given that competition is such a key feature of our contemporary economic system, Williams hints at the seeds of a considerably more radical Christian ethic.

Williams spells out the distinction between creation and Creator in terms that help us see how the doctrine of divine simplicity underlines God's unique identity as Creator. Williams demonstrates that the attributes of the God of classical theism

> far from being abstract and alien importations into a properly scriptural and/or experientially grounded theology, allow created existence its own integrity and dignity, and deliver us from a theology in which God is in danger of being seen simply as a very important or uniquely powerful agent in the universe competing with other agents in the universe for space or control.[36]

In doing so, Williams draws upon two sources that will help us in our exploration of the doctrine of God and Christian action. The first is the Anglican philosophical theologian Austin Farrer.[37] Williams takes from Farrer the notion that God and creation are fundamentally distinct. Being a creature who acts does not rule out God's action in the life of that creature even as that creature acts:

> The key is the realization that, whereas the typical act of one sort of finite nature cannot coexist with the act of another kind of finite nature, this cannot apply in the case of infinity: we cannot say that the finite excludes the infinite *in the way that* one finite agency excludes the other.[38]

In other words, God is not just another actor on the stage of creation. We might say, however, that God writes the play, provides the playhouse and the costumes and does all the casting himself. As such, Williams notes that 'to use infinite agency to close a gap is to rob it of its infinite character'.[39]

We do not say that we can see God acting here and here and here, playing this part in the cosmic play or making this or that cameo appearance. Instead, God as Creator holds the entirety of creation in being at any given created moment: 'what infinite agency causes simply is the system of secondary causality within which we finite agents act ... what it means for infinite causality/agency to be at work *is* that a system of finite causes is operating – not that a more impressive instance of finite causality is invoked to complete the picture'.[40] God is not *just* another actor in the play.

This notion of God as 'not another' is also found in the second source upon which Williams draws, the German theologian Nicholas of Cusa (1401–64). Williams takes over from Nicholas of Cusa the notion of God as *non aliud* or 'not another thing'.[41] This notion of God as 'not another' thing is important for any understanding of divine simplicity.

For Nicholas of Cusa, God is not another thing in the universe. However, nor is God that 'thing' in the universe which is not a thing (the only God-thing there is). Rather, God is simply God, he is 'not another'. To put this another way, God is outside the world of 'others' and things which he created.

In saying this Nicholas is drawing on a philosophical tradition stemming from the Greek philosopher Plato, known as Neo-Platonism, which stresses the absoluteness of the One or the divine over and against creation and the composite world of 'manys'.[42] Often the use of such thought by Christians has been criticized for being non-scriptural. However, the use of philosophical thought to illuminate a truth discovered in Scripture is distinct from deriving a 'truth' not found in Scripture from such philosophical thought. Christians who make use of philosophical thought as a means of articulating or interpreting Scripture are still using Scripture as their primary source of theological material and revelation.

Nicholas of Cusa makes use of Neo-Platonic thought while discussing the nature of God. He makes particular use of Pseudo-Dionysius, a Christian Neo-Platonist writing in the

fifth/sixth centuries CE.[43] Claudio D'Amico notes that along
with Plato and the pagan fifth-century Neo-Platonist Proclus
'all three of them are explicitly or implicitly present everywhere in his writings'.[44] Nicholas takes over from Dionysius
the notion that God is outside the created world of things.
Nicholas cites Pseudo-Dionysius as a source for his concept of
God as 'not another'. God '"is not thing and is not any other
thing; He is not here and is not there," as the same Dionysius
says regarding the divine names; for just as He is all things, so
He is not any of all the things'.[45]

Once again this affirmation is grounded in the doctrine of
creation.[46] As Creator, God exceeds all of the created order
by virtue of being its creator. Nicholas again cites Pseudo-
Dionysius: 'for, as Dionysius concludes at the end of *The
Mystical Theology*: "above all affirmation God is the perfect
and unique Cause of all things; and the excellence of Him who
is unqualifiedly free from all things and is beyond all things is
above the negation of all things"'.[47] God is not this *thing* or
not that *thing*; as their Creator he is completely outside the
networks of things that make up the world of things.

Werner Beierwalters notes that Nicholas's notion of God
as 'not another' puts God outside the world of differentiation
between things – beyond the world of 'this thing or that thing
but not this thing or not that thing' – while also relating God
intimately to everything that ever is. God as 'not another'
means that God is acting in that 'another' 'as its constituting
ground'.[48] God is the eternal 'other' which makes each created
instance of another 'this' or 'that' in the created order the
particular 'this' or 'that' which God is calling it to be. For
Nicholas, as Clyde Lee Miller notes, God is 'the ever-present
all-encompassing, yet independent divine source of all that is
not God but still dependent on God'.[49]

We have dealt at some length with the insight of Nicholas
of Cusa because I think it is one of the clearest formulations of
what is central to the affirmation of divine simplicity: that God
is Creator, that God is distinct from creation but intimately

involved in it as he holds it in being, and that God is nothing like any-*thing* we have experienced. Miller paraphrases Nicholas's insight well: 'the divine Not-Other is not one of the things we are familiar with in the world we inhabit, where all is multiplicity and difference'.[50] These insights help us to understand what divine simplicity seeks to affirm when applied to the doctrine of God.

Problems of Threeness: The Trinity

The doctrine of the Trinity is sometimes heralded as an argument against divine simplicity. Jordan Barrett, a defender of a somewhat modified account of divine simplicity, states that 'the Trinity seems to require greater distinctions than divine simplicity will allow'.[51] We do not have space here fully to articulate a doctrine of the Trinity in relation to divine simplicity. It is enough for us to point out that simplicity does not rule out the doctrine of the Trinity. It should be noted from the outset that proponents of classical theism do not propose divine simplicity without also simultaneously proposing that God is Trinity.[52]

Indeed, divine simplicity may have an important role to play in articulating a doctrine of the Trinity that affirms the oneness of God. A possible reason for the fall in popularity of divine simplicity within theological discourse is the corresponding rise in social trinitarianism within Trinitarian thought. Social trinitarianism highlights the threeness of the divine persons in community, and often draws a Christian ethic from that "threeness". Richard Muller describes this trend within modern doctrines of God. He notes:

> traditional understandings of God, both of the divine essence and attributes and of the Trinity, have been caricatured for the sake of replacing them with notions of a changing, temporal deity whose oneness is merely social ... [there is]

a radical misconstrual, whether intentional or unintentional of the traditional attributes, notably simplicity, immutability and eternity, done in the name of divine relationality.[53]

For example, Paul Hinlicky, who is critical of traditional divine simplicity and prefers a 'weak' account, repeatedly refers to the Trinity as the 'Beloved Community'.[54]

Social Trinitarianism rightly foregrounds the 'threeness' of the persons of the Holy Trinity and their relationship against an historical tendency to emphasize the 'oneness' of God to the point of rendering the notion of Trinity almost obsolete. The case against social Trinitarianism has been well made elsewhere.[55] For our purposes it is sufficient to note that the mystery of the Holy Trinity is precisely that God is *simultaneously* one *and* three, in a way that is beyond our conception or understanding because we know of nothing that can be *simultaneously* one *and* three. This is why all images of the Trinity are heretical and Trinity Sunday is (unfortunately) the least favoured of many preachers. Because of the limitations of our thought and speech, any articulation of the Trinity, however subtle, will tend to emphasize *either* the oneness *or* the threeness of the doctrine. The doctrine of the Trinity stands as a constant reminder that even the best doctrinal formulation is as nothing compared to the glorious mystery that is God.

While divine simplicity is sometimes ruled out on the grounds that it cannot be simultaneously maintained with a doctrine of the Trinity, Dolezal argues instead that the doctrine of the Trinity *requires* divine simplicity:

without divine simplicity, the Father, Son, and Holy Spirit potentially could be understood as three parts of God – in which case each person would lack something of the fullness of divinity – or as three discrete beings who collectively make up a social unit we call God.[56]

White agrees that any notion of divine unity is 'predicated upon some account of divine simplicity'.[57] Far from rendering the doctrine of the Trinity obsolete, divine simplicity may therefore be a safeguard against the potential of tritheism, dividing the Trinity into 'three gods' or bits of something called 'god'. Moreover, White suggests that divine simplicity prevents us from falsely projecting models of earthly unity on to the Godhead, even the highest forms of earthly unity such as the communion between created persons in the Church. 'To avoid such patent anthropomorphism', he writes, 'we stand in need of a doctrine of divine simplicity.'[58]

Problems of Oneness: The Identity of Attributes

Another common objection to divine simplicity is the identity of divine attributes that follows as a consequence of affirming divine simplicity. If God is simple, his attributes are identical and he is identical with his attributes. White puts this well: 'Whatever God's simplicity is, and we have no direct, immediate experience of it, it is identical with God's perfection, goodness and so forth.'[59]

According to divine simplicity, God's wisdom and God's anger are identical and he is identical with them. This also holds for attributes which seem contradictory to us, for example his mercy and his justice. We explore God's anger in chapter 4 below, and the mercy and justice of God in chapter 5.

Stephen Holmes is right to suggest some caution here to prevent our talk of God sliding into complete incoherence. The basis of the identity of divine attributes lies not so much in a claim about individual attributes (which the doctrine of divine simplicity says cannot be isolated within God) as in a claim about God himself. Aquinas, argues Holmes, 'insists that it is meaningful to assert that there is a foundation in God for our distinct conceptions of him, while insisting that this foundation is not any real division within his essence'.[60]

Aquinas deals with such attributes when considering divine simplicity. In his reply to objections against divine simplicity, he argues that 'virtue and wisdom are not predicated of God and of us univocally. Hence it does not follow that there are accidents in God as there are in us'.[61] Put more simply, whatever it means for us to be wise, it is different to what it means for God to be wise.

Many contemporary discussions of divine attributes assume that there must be a sense in which such divine attributes are related to their human counterpart in some way. They assume, for example, that divine anger must be like human anger for it be considered 'anger' at all. Aquinas meanwhile argues that anger is attributed to God on grounds of similarity of effect. God's 'anger' is the effect of God's action on those with whom he is 'angry': 'Anger and the like are attributed to God on account of a similitude of effect. Thus, because to punish is properly the act of an angry man, God's punishment is metaphorically spoken of as His anger.'[62] According to Aquinas, we call a human 'angry' because of a state they exhibit, but we call God 'angry' because the effects of God's action on the object of his anger resemble those caused by an angry person on the world around them.

Aquinas's hesitancy to identify human and divine attributes is both a recognition of the simplicity of God in contrast to the composite nature of creatures and their creaturely attributes, and also a guard against idolatry. It serves to prevent the idolatrous projection of creaturely concepts onto our understanding of God. White notes that 'definitions of God which begin from univocal terms drawn from material individuals are destined to be false starting points, potentially idolatrous concepts'.[63]

The danger of idolatry is a recurring theme that we will encounter at several places in the course of this book. Aquinas's concern here is that if we assume an attribute of God is the same as its corresponding human attribute, differing only in degree, we run into the danger of developing an idolatrous concept of God based on such human attributes. Instead of

God's nature being primary in our thoughts about God and our worship of him, we risk making our creaturely experience of those attributes primary. Our creaturely experience of such attributes in their created form means that we risk worshipping idolatrous pictures of God based on that experience. Our false projections of God become our primary focus, rather than the God who reveals himself to transcend all such creaturely limitations. This point was also made by St Gregory of Nyssa: 'every concept which comes from some comprehensible image by an approximate understanding and by guessing at the divine nature constitutes an idol of God and does not proclaim God'.[64] If we make our creaturely experience primary in our conception of God, we are never very far from the risk of idolatry. This is easier said than done, which is why our attention always needs to be refocused onto God himself.

Another common argument against divine simplicity is the difficulty in conceiving of the identity of attributes. If God is simple, then his attributes are identical. His mercy is identical with his anger and with his power and with his love, and so on. For some, the identity of attributes is so nonsensical as to be a conclusive argument against divine simplicity.[65] In part this criticism is founded on our creaturely experience of such attributes. Our anger is not our love. Our experience of power is not our experience of mercy, and so on. We have already seen the danger of making our experience of such attributes primary in declaring that what is distinct for us must also be distinct in God.

For others, the identity of attributes fails to do justice to the biblical witness to the nature and character of God, and the distinctiveness of God's attributes of anger, justice, mercy and so on that we seem to discover there. Barrett claims that such distinctions 'must be acknowledged in God and not just in the human mind ... because God has revealed himself to be this way in Scripture'.[66] However, the proponents of classical theism and defenders of the identity of God's attributes also hold that the simplicity of God is the way that God has revealed himself to be in Scripture.

Accounts which regard the identity of attributes as inconsistent with Scripture often run the danger of accusing proponents of classical theism of neglecting or misreading the Scriptures. Instead, Aquinas and Anselm find that the doctrine of divine simplicity and the identity of attributes arises out of their reading of Scripture. Holmes offers a particularly important corrective to those who deny divine simplicity on scriptural grounds. He argues that divine simplicity arises out of what we are able confidently to affirm or deny about God, based on his revelation of himself in Scripture:

> The particular human realities that we deny or extrapolate, of course, can only be discerned through a hearing of God's revelation: God denies his own mutability or transience in Scripture, but affirms that he is love, and so we may speak with confidence concerning these matters, at least, when we turn to simplicity, the basic affirmation of the oneness of God is certainly Scriptural.[67]

The identity of attributes doesn't tell us something strange about the identity of love and anger, it tells us something about the fundamental oneness of God. Attributes which appear in isolation in us cohere in God.

The identity of divine attributes is key to the argument of this book. One of the fruits of the doctrine of divine simplicity is that it enables us to hold together what initially appear to be contradictory attributes of God which we struggle to conceive together at the same time. Thus our understanding of God's love is informed by his wisdom, by his mercy, by his anger and so on because they are simply what it means to be God. Theologies with an overdeveloped focus on this or that attribute are likely to be bad theologies, as are theologies that neglect a corresponding seemingly contradictory divine attribute. For example, theologies that focus on the wrath of God to the exclusion of his love or the endless mercy of God to the exclusion of his righteous judgement.

The scriptural witness is more nuanced than such one-sided distortions. A preacher might only preach about God's anger at sinful and fallen humanity and our behaviour, but to do so would be to identify God solely with his anger and distort the Scriptures which also point to the God who redeems us out of love for us even in our fallen state. Alternatively, we might be misled, by singing hymns or worship songs that focus on the 'overwhelming, never-ending, reckless love of God'[68] and cause us to exclaim 'O love, how deep, how broad, how high!',[69] into thinking that God's love is laissez-faire, a licence for 'anything goes', without a corresponding focus on God's corrective judgement in Christ of all the human ways of being and patterns of injustice that fall short of that love.

Such disproportionate focuses on God's anger to the exclusion of his love, or his love to the exclusion of his judgement, are caricatures and yet we are all to some extent guilty of such distortions. Our understanding of God and his action tends towards one or other of God's attributes. The Gospel as we proclaim it focuses more on God's mercy and less on God's judgement, or vice versa. Our own particular emphasis might even change from time to time during the course of our Christian life. Here the identity of divine attributes helps us. Far from being a nonsensical obstacle, the identity of divine attributes suggested by divine simplicity is an important corrective to all such theological distortions. Divine simplicity helps us to hold together attributes in God that we struggle to conceive together within our human experience of similar attributes. The identity of attributes helps us keep our focus on God as the source and centre of our theology, and illuminates the distortions in our proclamation of the Gospel that inevitably creep in as we attempt to balance aspects of God's identity that appear contradictory in creatures.

This is one fruit of the doctrine of divine simplicity. To act in accordance with this understanding of God is to consistently refine our speech and refocus our attention on God. It requires us to consider whether our thinking about God is in line with the whole of God's nature revealed to us in Scripture. It guards against the natural tendency to choose to favour one side of God's nature over what seems at first glance to be an opposing characteristic or attribute.

There are other fruits of the doctrine of divine simplicity in how we live the Christian life. Our final chapter is devoted to exploring what the Christian life might look like if lived in accordance with the pattern given to us when we consider the nature of God according to classical theism as a whole. At this moment we can point to the implications for Christian action that arise in the light of divine simplicity. Divine simplicity, and especially the identity of attributes, reveal to us that God's action and attributes are perfectly integrated and unified. In contrast, as composite creatures who are anything but simple, divine simplicity reminds us that as creatures our actions reveal different aspects of ourselves to be segregated and disunited. For example, what we say we do and what we actually do come apart. We claim to be people who care for justice or the common good, yet we contribute to structures of injustice through indifference. We say our relationship with God is at the centre of our lives, yet we spend little time in prayer or communion with God.

Reflecting on divine simplicity as it reveals to us God's unity and the identity of his attributes shows us where our creatureliness has become distorted. Caution is needed here. As creatures, especially creatures made in God's image, we are not called to rid ourselves of those different aspects of our being which make us the creatures God is calling us to be. As composite creatures we are not called to become 'simple'. Indeed, that would be impossible. Instead, divine simplicity challenges us to think about the various aspects of ourselves and the extent to which they are united and integrated within a fully harmonious and holistic human life.

Divine simplicity challenges our tendency to compartmentalize ourselves and to distort our ways of thinking and being. It encourages us to think through *all* that we actually think and say and do and to ask whether each and every aspect of ourselves is truly serving the one who called us into being. Are we focusing on one aspect of our life to the exclusion of all others? Has our focus on work to support our family eclipsed our focus on the very family we work to support? Has our desire for a career caused us to lay aside causes and principles we hold dear? Are we focusing on those around us and people like us to the exclusion of others who cross our paths, of whom we may not be aware? Are we heeding God's call to integration or subscribing to a distorted narrative of ourselves given to us by others?

The remainder of this book focuses on different attributes of the God of classical theism. In this light, we now turn to explore the nature of God revealed to us in Scripture according to the proponents of classical theism. We begin by reflecting on whether it is possible for God to suffer, and what this means for our redemption from suffering achieved in Christ.

Notes

1 Irenaeus of Lyons, *Against Heresies* 2.13.3; available at: www.newadvent.org/fathers/0103213.htm (accessed 13.8.19).

2 Behr, J. 'Synchronic and Diachronic Harmony: St. Irenaeus on Divine Simplicity', in *Modern Theology* 35.3 (July 2019), pp. 428–41, 428.

3 Anselm, *Proslogion* XVIII, trans. Charlesworth, M. J. (Oxford: Clarendon Press 1965).

4 Wolterstorff, N. 'Divine Simplicity', in *Philosophical Perspectives, Vol. 5, Philosophy of Religion* (1991), pp. 531–52.

5 Dolezal, J. E., ' Review of Duby. S., *Divine Simplicity: A Dogmatic Account*. T&T Clark Studies in Systematic Theology (London: Bloomsbury T&T Clark, 2016)', in *Pro Ecclesia* XXVI.4 (2017), pp. 463–7, 463.

6 White, T. J., 'Divine Simplicity and the Holy Trinity', in *International Journal of Systematic Theology* 18.1 (January 2016), pp. 66–93, 67; see also Holmes, S. R., 'Something Much Too Plain to Say: Towards a Defence of the Doctrine of Divine Simplicity', in *Neue Zeitschrift*

für Systematische Theologie und Religionsphilosophie 43.1 (2001), pp. 137–54.

7 Barrett, J. P., 'Review of *Divine Simplicity: A Dogmatic Account. By Steven J. Duby.* T & T Clark Studies in Systematic Theology, 30', in *Theological Studies* 77(4) (December 2016), pp. 999–1000, 999.

8 See for example Duby, S. J., *Divine Simplicity: A Dogmatic Account* (London: T&T Clark, 2016); Dolezal, J. E., *All That Is In God: Evangelical Theology and the Challenge of Classical Christian Theism* (Grand Rapids, MI: Reformation Heritage Books, 2017); Dolezal, J. E., *God Without Parts: Divine Simplicity and the Metaphysics of God's Absoluteness* (Eugene, OR: Pickwick Publications, 2011).

9 See for example Barrett, J. P., *Divine Simplicity: A Biblical and Trinitarian Account* (Minneapolis: Fortress Press, 2017); Hinlicky, P. R., *Divine Simplicity: Christ the Crisis of Metaphysics* (Grand Rapids, MI: Baker Academic, 2016).

10 White, 'Divine Simplicity', p. 90.

11 White, 'Divine Simplicity', pp. 70–1.

12 For the limits of apophaticism in Aquinas's concept of simplicity see Burns, R. M., 'The Divine Simplicity', in *Religious Studies* 25.3 (Sept 1989), pp. 271–93, 272; cf. White, 'Divine Simplicity', p. 71.

13 White, 'Divine Simplicity', p. 84.

14 White, 'Divine Simplicity', p. 84.

15 White, 'Divine Simplicity', p. 84.

16 Dolezal, *Without Parts*, p. 29. Likewise, Holmes, 'Much Too Plain', p. 153: 'If it is accepted that God's essence is incomprehensible … most of the theological problems that divine simplicity apparently raises can be side-stepped'.

17 Dolezal, *Without Parts*, p. 29.

18 White, 'Divine Simplicity', p. 84. See also Davies, B. 'Classical Theism and the Doctrine of Divine Simplicity', in Davies, B. (ed.), *Language, Meaning and God: Essays in Honour of Herbert McCabe OP* (London: Geoffrey Chapman 1987), pp. 51–74, especially 58–60.

19 Wolterstorff, 'Simplicity', p. 540.

20 Ward, K., 'The God of the Philosophers and the God of Abraham, Isaac, and Jacob', in *The Journal of Jewish Thought and Philosophy* 8 (1999), pp. 157–70, 158–9.

21 Ward, 'Philosophers', p. 159. Here we see why simplicity entails eternity: 'or time by its very nature contains parts, past, present and future, which are distinct and divided from one another. In the divine being there is no time, but all that to us is past, present or future is held together, perfectly possessed, in undivided consciousness' (Ward, 'Philosophers', p. 158).

22 Davies, 'Theism', p. 70.

23 Irenaeus, *Against Heresies* 2.13.3.

24 For the prevalence of gnosticism today see von Balthasar, H., 'Introduction', in *The Scandal of the Incarnation: Irenaeus Against the Heresies* (San Francisco: Ignatius Press, 1990), pp. 1–11.

25 Irenaeus, *Against Heresies* 2.13.3.

26 Irenaeus, *Against Heresies* 2.13.3.

27 For parallels between *Against Heresies* 2.13.3 and the Greek philosophical monotheist Xenophanes see Behr, 'Divine Simplicity', p. 428.

28 Irenaeus, *Against Heresies* 2.13.3.

29 Irenaeus, *Against Heresies* 4.11.2; see Behr, 'Divine Simplicity', p. 438.

30 Irenaeus, *Against Heresies* 4.11.2.

31 See especially *Summa Theologica* I.3; available at www.newadvent.org/summa/1003.htm (accessed 13.8.19).

32 Williams, R., *Christ the Heart of Creation* (London: Bloomsbury Continuum, 2018), p. 7.

33 For a clear presentation of Aquinas's argument here see: Lamont, J., 'Aquinas on Divine Simplicity', in *The Monist* 80.4 (Oct 1997), pp. 521–38, especially 531.

34 Aquinas, *Summa* 1.3.3.

35 Williams, *Heart of Creation*, p. xiii.

36 Williams, *Heart of Creation*, p. 11.

37 Williams draws primarily on Farrer, A., *Finite and Infinite: A Philosophical Essay* (London: Dacre Press 1943/New York: Seabury Press, 1979) and Farrer, A., *The Glass of Vision* (London: Dacre Press, 1948).

38 Williams, *Heart of Creation*, p. 4.

39 Williams, *Heart of Creation*, p. 2.

40 Williams, *Heart of Creation*, p. 2.

41 For a particularly clear exposition of Nicholas's dialogue devoted to his conception of God as 'not-other' see Miller, C. L., 'God as *Li Non-Aliud*: Nicholas of Cusa's Unique Designation for God', in *Journal of Medieval Religious Cultures* 41.1 (2015), pp. 24–49.

42 For the reception and interpretation of Platonism by Nicholas de Cusa see D'Amico, C., 'Plato and the Platonic Tradition in the Philosophy of Nicholas of Cusa', in Kim, A., *Brill's Companion to German Platonism* (Leiden: Brill, 2019), pp. 15–43. See also Beierwalters, W., 'Centrum tocius vite: The Significance of Proclus's *Theologia Platonis* in the Thought of Nicholas Cusanus', in *Yearbook of the Irish Philosophical Society* (2000), pp. 141–56; Gersh, S., 'Nicholas of Cusa', in *Interpreting Proclus: From Antiquity to Renaissance* (Cambridge: Cambridge University Press, 2014), pp. 318–52; and Adamson, P., Karfik, F., 'Proclus' Legacy', in d'Hoine, P., Martijn, M., *All From One: A Guide to Proclus* (Oxford: Oxford University Press, 2017),

pp. 290–321. For the historical context of Aquinas's understanding of simplicity, and the influence of Neoplatonic thought, see Burns, 'Simplicity'. For other Greek philosophical influences on the development of simplicity see Stead, C., 'Divine Simplicity as a Problem for Orthodoxy', in Williams, R., *The Making of Orthodoxy: Essays in Honour of Henry Chadwick* (Cambridge: Cambridge University Press, 1989), pp. 255–69. However, Stead overstates the case that simplicity is borrowed from certain schools of philosophy and underestimates the extent to which it is possible to derive divine simplicity from reflection on Scripture.

43 Pseudo-Dionysius writes in the guise of Dionysius the Areopagite referred to in Acts 17.34.

44 D'Amico, 'Platonic Tradition', p. 21.

45 Nicholas of Cusa, *De dicta ignorantia* I.16, in Hopkins, J. (trans.), *Nicholas of Cusa on Learned Ignorance: A Translation and Appraisal of De docta ignorantia* (Minneapolis: Banning Press, 1981), p. 25 (available at jasper-hopkins.info/DI-I-12-2000.pdf; accessed 13.6.19), citing Pseudo-Dionysius, *The Divine Names* 5 (*Dionysiaca* I, pp. 355–6). For the same in Thomas Aquinas see White, 'Divine Simplicity', p. 76.

46 Beierwalters notes that Nicholas of Cusa's insight is to connect the absoluteness of the One of Neoplatonism 'in a conceptually convincing manner, with the trinitarian self-constitution of God and with his role as creator' (Beierwalters, 'Significance', p. 143).

47 Nicholas of Cusa, *De dicta ignorantia* I.16, citing Pseudo-Dionysius, *The Mystical Theology* 5 (*Dionysiaca* I, pp. 601–2).

48 Beierwalters, 'Significance', p. 149.

49 Miller, '*Non-Aliud*', pp. 28–9.

50 Miller, '*Non-Aliud*', p. 30.

51 Barrett, 'Divine Simplicity', pp. 171–2.

52 Stephen Holmes suggests that the modern difficulty in asserting simplicity with Trinity might suggest that simplicity is being misunderstood: 'If the problems of reconciling the concept of simplicity with the triune God of Scripture are as obvious as we have been led to think in recent years, someone in this tradition should have noticed, and the apparent fact that nobody did suggests that the modern problems are a result of a misunderstanding of the tradition somewhere' (Holmes, 'Much Too Plain', p. 140, see also pp. 147–9).

53 Muller, R., 'Foreword', in Dolezal, *All That Is In God*, pp. ix–xii, ix, xi.

54 Hinlicky, *Simplicity*, p. xi: 'the Three who are Beloved Community'.

55 See especially Chapman, M. D., 'The Social Doctrine of the Trinity: Some Problems', in *Anglican Theological Review* 83.2 (2001), pp. 239–54; Kilby, K., 'Perichoresis and Projection: Problems with

Social Doctrines of the Trinity', in *New Blackfriars* 81 (1957), pp. 432–45.

56 Dolezal, *All That Is In God*, p. 105. White, 'Divine Simplicity', pp. 70–1, also notes: 'divine simplicity matters greatly for trinitarian theology, and needs to be recovered in depth, in view of a deeper reflection on the balance and coherence of trinitarian thought'.

57 White, 'Divine Simplicity', p. 90.

58 White, 'Divine Simplicity', p. 90.

59 White, 'Divine Simplicity', p. 81.

60 Holmes, 'Much Too Plain', p. 143.

61 *Summa Theologica* I.3.6.

62 *Summa Theologica* I.3.2.

63 White, 'Divine Simplicity', p. 76.

64 Gregory of Nyssa, *Life of Moses*, trans. Malherbe, A., Ferguson, E. (New York: Paulist Press, 1978), pp. 95–6.

65 For example, Plantinga, A., *Does God Have a Nature?* (Milwaukee: Marquette University Press, 1980).

66 Barrett, *Simplicity*, p. 183.

67 Holmes, 'Much Too Plain', pp. 150–1.

68 Asbury, C. 'Reckless Love', in album *Reckless Love* (Redding, CA: Bethel, 2018).

69 Webb, B. (trans.), 'O love, how deep, how broad, how high', in *The Hymnal Noted* (London: J. A. Novello, 1854) (from the fifteenth-century Latin of Thomas à Kempis, *O amor quam extaticus*).

2

The Suffering of God

This is the decisive difference between Christianity and all religions. Man's religiosity makes him look in his distress to the power of God in the world; he uses God as a deus ex machina. The Bible, however, directs us to the powerlessness and suffering of God; only a suffering God can help. (Dietrich Bonhoeffer)[1]

In discussions of the classical attributes of God, whereas simplicity is often ignored, divine impassibility (God's inability to suffer) is often vehemently rejected. Perhaps no other area of the doctrine of God has changed so fundamentally from the widespread assumption that God cannot suffer, to the widespread assumption within the theology of the last century that he must.

The question of whether God can suffer tends to generate passionate responses. This is understandable, since the assertion of God being liable to suffering is a response to the very real and traumatic suffering occurring in our world even now. It is because of the depths of human depravity and suffering experienced in the twentieth century that the notion of the passibility of God (his ability to suffer) has gained such widespread support. The trauma of mass genocide such as that witnessed in Auschwitz led inevitably to the question: 'Where is God in this?' As a result, the depths of suffering in this world were transferred eternally to God. Kenneth Surin was by no means alone when he said: 'the only credible theology for Auschwitz is one that makes God an inmate of the place'.[2] The theology of Jürgen Moltmann (born 1926) will be a central focus of this chapter. His account of God's nature developed out of his experiences of the Second World War: 'Shattered and broken, the survivors of my generation were then returning from camps and hospitals to the lecture room. A theology which did not speak of God in the sight of one who was abandoned and crucified would have had nothing to say to us then.'[3]

We shall argue that in the face of suffering what is needed is not a change in our doctrine of God, but careful attention to what God does in the face of suffering. Further, we shall argue that contemporary trends within theology that suggest that God must suffer (and is therefore passible) do not ultimately achieve what they set out to achieve. What is required is not a suffering God, but an impassible God who does not suffer suffering but rather transforms it in Christ, and calls us to do likewise. In the words of Paul Gavrilyuk: 'in order to be redemptive God's involvement in suffering must be marked by impassibility'.[4]

This chapter continues laying the theological groundwork we began to set down in the first chapter for the argument of this book as a whole. The remaining chapters become more practical and focused on how our action may be informed in the light of God's nature and action in the world. We shall argue here that, in line with divine simplicity, divine impassibility as a feature of classical theism should be affirmed. Considering the suffering of God provides us with a gateway into thinking about Christian action in the light of God, because it focuses us on what needs to change in us, or rather the change in human society in which we need to participate in order to make our action share in the transformative action of God against suffering in the world.

The God of classical theism is impassible, he is incapable of suffering. This is related to his immutability (his inability to change). The God in whom 'there is no variation or shadow due to change' (James 1.17) is not liable to change, and therefore not liable to suffering. However, we read in Scripture that on the road to Emmaus the Risen Jesus says to his two followers: 'Oh, how foolish you are, and how slow of heart to believe all that the prophets have declared! Was it not necessary that the Messiah should suffer these things and then enter into his glory?' (Luke 24.25-26).

'The Messiah should suffer.' We know that the Cross is at the centre of the Christian faith. We have as one of our central motifs the image of a man undergoing prolonged and excruciating suffering. Theologies get themselves into trouble if the Cross ceases to occupy this central place – but they also get themselves into trouble when the Cross is abstracted from the whole of the life of that man, the life of God himself. The Cross isn't the arbitrary suffering of one man for all of us. The Cross is the means by which we put to death the human life of the living God himself. The whole of that human life of God is the basis of all our theology, not just its end.

And it's not just the end of that life that raises questions for the doctrine of divine impassibility. It's not just his death that raises questions about whether we can still say that God is incapable of suffering. The whole of his life as one of us forces this question. All of us know, some of us too well, that human beings suffer. We are liable to hurt and change. We grow, age, and feel pain. If God is one of us in Christ, as we know him to be, God in Christ suffers. We've put our fingers on one of those tensions which Christian orthodoxy seems frustratingly happy to let be. The impassible God suffers in Christ. The suffering of the impassible and immutable God is the central paradox of the Christian faith.

Over the course of the twentieth century, suffering has no longer been proclaimed as something that the impassible God defeats in Christ, but something that occurs in his very self. Gavrilyuk notes the extent to which the impassible God was ridiculed as '"the celestial Narcissus," "the self-protecting monarch," "the patriarchal ruler," "the eternal by-stander" ... and numerous other non-flattering appellations'.[5] While calling for an end to such 'divine name-calling', Gavrilyuk pulls no punches in return: 'I suppose traditional theists could return the compliment by calling the God of modern passibilism The Perpetual Heavenly Masochist ...The Idol of Self-Flagellating Theological Liberalism, or The Grand Phantasm of Victimhood Ideology (take your pick).'[6]

Moltmann is the most famous modern proponent of a passible God who suffers in his very being. The litmus test of theology is often what it means for our salvation. In this chapter, and elsewhere, we will find that Moltmann's theological account of Christ's suffering is severely lacking in its ability to account for how it is we are saved *from* suffering *through* Christ's suffering. However, in our final chapter, we shall see that Moltmann has important things to say to us about what it means to act as Christians in the world, even if his doctrine of God somewhat misses the mark.

Moltmann attempts to reverse the traditional theological focus on what God in Christ means for us and for our salvation. He is explicit about this: 'I reversed the question. What does the cross of Christ mean for God? Does an impassible God keep silent in heaven untouched by the suffering and death of his child on Golgotha?'[7]

However, we need to observe carefully what Moltmann is doing here. This is not a simple reversal of the question posed by classical theism. Moltmann's reversed question has been glossed in terms that fundamentally weaken the relations between the persons of the Trinity.[8] No longer are we dealing with the nature of God: Father, Son and Spirit. Instead, Moltmann asks us to consider the consequences on the nature of God for the death of the Son, without sufficient reference to their unity. He repeatedly divides 'God' and the 'Son' in describing the events of the Cross: 'The death of the Son of God on the cross reaches deep into the nature of God and, above all other meanings, is an event which takes place in the innermost nature of God himself: the fatherless Son and the sonless Father.'[9]

In Christian orthodoxy, Father and Son are relational terms that point to the Son's being eternally begotten of the Father. Moltmann therefore drives a coach and horses through the doctrine of the eternal generation in God of the Son from the Father.

It is as a result of the fourth-century Arian crisis that Christian orthodoxy discovered this way of speaking of the relation between Father and Son. The Arian crisis came about through the dispute with Arius (died 336 CE), for whom the Son was a creature and not God by nature. In order to maintain his divinity Christian orthodoxy asserts that the Son is not a creature. The Son is on the creator side of the creator/creation distinction we traced above. So, for example, Cyril of Jerusalem (c. 315–86 CE): 'the Son of God, the one and only, our Lord Jesus Christ, who is God begotten of God, who is life begotten of life, who is light begotten of light, who is in all things like unto the begetter, and who did not come to exist in time but was before all the ages, eternally and incomprehensibly begotten of the Father'.[10]

Moltmann overlooks the eternal generation of the Son from the Father, separating the Son from the Father at the moment of crucifixion. At other points, Moltmann seems to remove God from the scene of the crucifixion altogether: 'either Jesus who was abandoned by God is the end of all theology or he is the beginning of a specifically Christian and therefore critical and liberating theology and life'.[11]

To see the crucifixion as only a moment of abandonment and failure is to forget the entirety of Christian theological speculation since that first Easter Day. We have already seen Luke's account of the encounter on the Road to Emmaus. The disciples, who see the Cross as a scene of failure, are taught the necessity of the Messiah's suffering as a means to glory (Luke 24.26). In Paul's preaching the Cross remains scandalous to Jews and foolish to Gentiles, but to those who are Christian it is a sign of God's power: 'For God's foolishness is wiser than human wisdom, and God's weakness is stronger than human strength.' (1 Cor. 1.24–5).[12]

To view the crucifixion only as an act of abandonment of Jesus by God, or the Son by the Father, reveals the problematic Christology and Trinitarianism that runs throughout Moltmann's thought. If the abandonment of Jesus by God is pursued, Jesus is no longer the human life of the divine Word. At times Moltmann's language divides Christ's humanity from his divinity so strongly that he seems to separate them completely. For example, 'Does God simply allow Christ to suffer for us? Or does God himself suffer in Christ on our behalf?'[13]

On the other hand, if Moltmann's abandonment of the Son by the Father is pursued, the Trinity is divided and the fundamental unity of action of Father, Son, and Holy Spirit is disturbed. We saw above how an account of something like divine simplicity is necessary to safeguard the unity of the Trinity.[14] While it is the case that only the Son is united to humanity in Christ, the unity of action of the three persons means that we can say that the whole of humanity is united to the whole of divinity through the incarnation of the Son.

Our focus in this chapter is the extent to which we can say that God is liable to suffering and change. While classical theism asserts that God cannot suffer or change, the extent to which Moltmann ascribes change within the Godhead can be seen in such passages as: 'The incarnation of the Son therefore brings about something "new" even within the Trinity, for God himself. After the Son's return the relationship between the Father and the Son is no longer entirely the same.'[15] To use the language of 'return' in respect of the Incarnation is deeply problematic as it both promotes the idea of the Incarnation as a kind of supernatural visit from a deity on high, and also disrupts the fundamental unity between Father, Son (and Spirit) during the Incarnation. The promise that anyone who has seen Christ has seen the Father (John 14.9) is just one instance in Scripture which reminds us of the continued unity of the Father and the Son in the Incarnation.

Lying behind this ascription of change to the Trinity is Moltmann's abandonment of another attribute of the God of classical theism, namely his eternity, which we touched upon in the previous chapter. Classical theism maintains that the whole of the temporal order and notions of 'past, present and future' are located *within* creation. God as Creator remains 'outside' of time as the eternal 'he who is'.[16] Moltmann meanwhile is clear: 'time's "beforehand-afterwards" structure has to be carried into the divine eternity as well; and we have to talk about a divine nature before this decision and a divine nature after it'.[17] He has strong reasons for suggesting there is a temporal structure within God because he wants to appeal the history between the persons of the Trinity: 'The concrete "history of God" in the death of Jesus on the cross of Golgotha therefore contains within itself all the depths and abysses of human history and therefore can be understood as the history of history.'[18] This raises similar problems to the 'oneness' of the three persons of the Trinity through the abandonment of an eternal relationship between Father and Son, and once again blurs the distinction between Creator and creation. Moreover, Moltmann's grounds for doing so are almost always given as the rejection of a philosophical concept of God that has corrupted the Biblical witness: 'The intellectual bar to this came from the philosophical concept of God, according to which God's being is incorruptible, unchangeable, indivisible, incapable of suffering and immortal.'[19]

It is now time to address one of the most commonplace accusations against the God of classical theism, that it is the result of a philosophical corruption rather than a product of the scriptural witness. This accusation is levelled against the traditional divine attributes more often than it is argued, and explains something of the ease with which Moltmann is willing to abandon the impassibility of God. Moltmann insists:

> We must drop the philosophical axioms about the nature of God. God is *not unchangeable*, if to be unchangeable means that he could not in the freedom of his love open himself to the changeable history of his creation. God is *not incapable*

of suffering if this means that in the freedom of his love he would not be receptive to suffering over the contradiction of man and the self-destruction of his creation. God is not invulnerable if this means that he could not open himself to the pain of the cross. God is *not perfect* if this means that he did not in the craving of his love want his creation to be necessary to his perfection.[20]

He rejects the traditional attributes of classical theism as 'philosophical axioms'.

Moltmann's rejection of the perfection of God without reference to creation is especially problematic. He seems to be making creation necessary to God's perfection.[21] Here is an example of the initial attractiveness of a potential position having profound consequences further down the theological line. By making creation necessary for the perfection of God, Moltmann both renders God imperfect 'before' or 'without' creation, and robs creation of its character as gift.[22] Creation becomes a necessary means to bring about God's perfection, rather than the utterly free gift of a God who does not need to create us. God may also no longer be free if he requires creation for his own perfection.

In the case of God's ability to change (mutability) and God's ability to suffer (passibility) Moltmann affirms these as a means of ensuring God has a loving relationship with creation. Classical theism maintains that God's inability to suffer or to change does not inhibit a loving relationship with his creation. Moltmann affirms the mutability and passibility of God on two grounds. Firstly, because he thinks that the philosophical intrusion of classical theism into Christian faith requires God to be 'apathetic', and by this he understands divine 'apathy' as requiring God to remain distant and unmoved. Secondly, he thinks that the language of paradox which classical theism draws upon to explain the mystery of the Cross is a helpless contradiction.

We can see both of these objections at play in the following passage:

Christian theology acquired Greek philosophy's ways of thinking in the Hellenistic world; and since that time most theologians have simultaneously maintained the passion of Christ, God's Son, and the deity's essential incapacity for suffering – even though it was at the price of having to talk paradoxically about 'the sufferings of the God who cannot suffer'. But in doing so they have simply added together Greek philosophy's 'apathy' axiom and the central statements of the Gospel. The contradiction remains – and remains unsatisfactory.[23]

In his *The Suffering of the Impassible God*, Gavrilyuk has demonstrated that both of Moltmann's objections are based on flawed assumptions about the supposed 'apathy' of the God of classical theism and, more importantly, on the philosophical intrusion of the divine attributes into Christian faith. Gavrilyuk notes that divine impassibility is often rejected as philosophical apathy 'without any serious analysis of its actual function in the thought of the Fathers ... [as] a convenient polemical starting point for the subsequent elaboration of a passibilist position'.[24]

Gavrilyuk rejects the notion that early Church theologies were 'held captive to the Greek philosophical concept of divine impassibility and simply failed to recognize that it stands in stark contrast to the Christian revelation'.[25] Instead, Gavrilyuk demonstrates that divine impassibility was not an unthinking adoption of Greek philosophy but an intentional

clearing of the decks of popular theological discourse to make space for God-befitting emotionally coloured characteristics such as mercy, love, and compassion ... divine impassibility meant first of all that God is in total control of his actions and that morally objectionable emotions are alien to him.[26]

It should be noted that proponents of classical theism base their doctrine of God not on Greek philosophy but the witness of Scripture itself. God's eternity and his simplicity are seen as part of the revelation of Scripture, not as an addition to it.[27] For example, we find the eternity of God in contrast to the temporality of his creation:

> Long ago you laid the foundation of the earth, and the heavens are the work of your hands. They will perish, but you endure; they will all wear out like a garment. You change them like clothing, and they pass away; but you are the same, and your years have no end. (Ps. 102.25–27)[28]

Elsewhere, he is described as 'eternal' (Gen. 21.33).[29] Psalm 136 repeatedly affirms 'his steadfast love endures for ever', and so on.

At this point it is important to note a distinction that is often in the background of those who posit the intrusion of Greek (or Hellenistic) ways of thinking onto Christian biblical faith. In the course of Christian theological scholarship, almost certainly under the influence of Christian anti-semitism, there arose the notion of a hard and fast division between the sophisticated thought of the Greeks (Hellenism) and the correspondingly simple faith of the Jewish or biblical world view. In this division, the New Testament was seen as a non-legalistic refinement of the biblical revelation. Martin Hengel was the scholar who finally rid Christian scholarship of this notion of a hard and fast division between Hellenism and Judaism.[30] He demonstrated that Judaism was hellenized following the spread of Greek culture in the Ancient Near East long before the writing of our New Testament. The fact of our New Testament being written in Greek should have alerted scholarship to this realization much earlier. Maintaining the notion of divine impassibility as a philosophical Greek adulteration of Christian biblical revelation serves to perpetuate this distinction if it is argued without sufficient care.

If suggesting a distinctive Greek philosophical concept of God implies a caricature of biblical thought, Gavrilyuk shows that the same is true of the Greek philosophical concept it implies. He argues that the concept of 'a single impassible philosophical deity disinterested in the world ... is a scholarly caricature, a convenient straw man put together by the modern proponent of the Theory of the Fall Into Hellenistic Philosophy'.[31]

Instead, Gavrilyuk demonstrates that the assertion of divine impassibility is a result of affirming the distinction between Creator and creature, which we saw above was also vital to the doctrine of divine simplicity: 'the question of worthy and unworthy divine emotions was not generated by alien philosophical convictions, but by the biblical idea that God, as creator, is different from everything created'.[32] As we found in our previous chapter, the attributes of classical theism are grounded in this fundamental distinction. Gavrilyuk finds the same is true for divine impassibility as 'first of all an ontological term, expressing God's unlikeness to everything created, his transcendence and supremacy over all things, rather than a psychological term implying the absence of emotion'.[33]

As in the case of divine simplicity, divine impassibility is an assertion that God lies outside the created order and it says as much about what God is *not*. Robert Jenson, while not a proponent of divine impassibility, makes an important observation in relation to divine impassibility as a feature of negative or apophatic theology. God not only transcends creaturely limits as Creator, which classical theism underlines again and again. God also transcends the negation of them: 'God to be sure transcends any conceivable "linear" time – as the partisans of divine impassibility rightly insist. And by the same token he also transcends any conceivable mere negation of our times – the negation on which partisans of divine impassibility seem to insist.'[34]

Like divine simplicity, divine impassibility affirms the fundamental distinction between God as Creator and creation. Gavrilyuk underscores this in a passage worth quoting in full:

Creatures are finite, visible, and passible; God, in contrast, is infinite, invisible, and impassible. One should beware of overinterpreting this contrast in the sense of 'detached', 'apathetic', and 'unemotional'. There is no warrant for such an interpretation in the sources. The idea expressed is fairly general and modest: God is unlike anything else, and therefore he acts and suffers action in a manner different from everything else.[35]

The Problem of Evil

As we saw in the introduction to this chapter, the passibility of God is often affirmed in the face of the very real evil and suffering that exists in the world. Those who defend the impassibility of God therefore need to be extremely sensitive in their rejection of God's passibility so that they do not belittle the very real suffering which is the concern of those who posit a God who is liable to suffering. Equally, however, those who suggest that God suffers cannot simply assume that those who defend an impassible God are insensitive or blind to the very great depths of suffering in the world. Richard Bauckham notes that the doctrine of divine impassibility flourished during a period of great suffering by the Church in the early experience of martyrdom.[36] As we shall see, in the face of such suffering maintaining God's impassibility can itself be the bedrock of a response to that suffering. The God of classical theism, while impassible, is not indifferent to suffering. A focus on the impassible God of classical theism can generate the kind of action in us that begins to transform the world and to tackle those areas of suffering and injustice to which modern defenders of the passibility of God have rightly drawn our attention. By witnessing God's own action in relation to such suffering, we can begin to formulate our response to it wherever it occurs.

We discussed the nature of heresy in our introduction. We saw how one frequent feature of heretical forms of thinking is that they seem to be the more obvious option when viewed in isolation or to make an aspect of Christian faith seem easier to swallow, while causing problems further down the theological line. Affirming God's ability to suffer gives us one example of such a pattern of thinking. It is easy to see the appeal of a passible God who suffers with the very real suffering in the world. However, maintaining that God is passible and able to suffer has considerable consequences for the question of how God redeems suffering.

Once again soteriology – how God saves us – is an important litmus test. Classical theism has taught that God's last word on suffering is his overcoming of it *because* he is impassible. He confronts death and redeems suffering through his death on the Cross because his impassibility means that he cannot be victim to suffering. Instead he encounters suffering and transforms it. In the famous words of St John Chrysostom:

> Let no one fear death, for the Death of our Saviour has set us free. He has destroyed it by enduring it. He destroyed Hell when He descended into it. He put it into an uproar even as it tasted of His flesh. Isaiah foretold this when he said, 'You, O Hell, have been troubled by encountering Him below.' Hell was in an uproar because it was done away with. It was in an uproar because it is mocked. It was in an uproar, for it is destroyed. It is in an uproar, for it is annihilated. It is in an uproar, for it is now made captive. Hell took a body, and discovered God. It took earth, and encountered Heaven.[37]

Maintaining a passible God who *can* suffer raises considerable questions about how God redeems suffering and brings about the salvation at the heart of our faith. In theologies that promote the passibility of God, God is often reduced to a fellow-traveller who undergoes suffering with us, while it remains unclear how it is that God saves us from this suffering, if at all. God's empathy with and understanding of earthly suffering is raised above God's transformation and redemption of the causes and situations of suffering. The transcendence of God in the face of suffering is reduced to companionship in suffering. Alfred Whitehead probably best articulates this view: 'God is the great companion – the fellow-sufferer who understands.'[38]

Gavrilyuk credits Cyril of Alexandria (c. 376–444 CE) with the realization that the paradox of the impassible God's suffering for our redemption 'lay at the very nerve centre of the Gospel'[39]:

> The Word who is above suffering in his own nature suffered by appropriating human nature and obtained victory over suffering. The celebration of this paradox in the creeds and hymns is the crowning achievement of a distinctly Christian account of divine involvement, an account for which no school of philosophy may take credit.[40]

Cyril famously defended the title of 'Mother of God' as an appropriate title for the Virgin Mary against his opponent Nestorius (born after 351–died after 451 CE), who claimed that we can only refer to Mary as mother of the human Christ. Cyril says that if we believe that Christ is God (and in Christ there is the mysterious unity of humanity and divinity), it follows that Mary is the Mother of God, in the sense that she bore the divine Christ into the world. This is not a debate about Mary but about how exactly Christ is simultaneously human and divine.[41] While for Nestorius humanity and divinity exists 'alongside' each other, for Cyril it is essential to say that one and the same Christ is both human and divine. Cyril asserted this not only because he realized who Christ is, but also because he realized the necessity of God suffering for us in Christ in order to bring about our redemption. He recognized that it is crucial for our salvation that it is as both human and divine that Christ undergoes suffering and death for our sake. It is necessary for our redemption that the God who is only life tastes death, because only his life can defeat death. Only he who cannot suffer can transform suffering for us by his suffering in Christ. This is put in its most stark form in

Cyril's famous twelfth anathema: 'the Word of God suffered in the flesh ... in that same flesh he tasted death and ... he is become the first-begotten of the dead, for, as he is God, he is the life and it is he that giveth life'.[42] Cyril repeatedly affirms the suffering in Christ of the one who is unable to suffer in relation to the purpose of that suffering – for our redemption:

> the Word of God is by nature immortal and incorruptible, and life and life-giving; since, however, his own body did, as Paul says, by the grace of God taste death for every man, he himself is said to have suffered death for us, not as if he had any experience of death in his own nature (for it would be madness to say or think this), but because, as I have just said, his flesh tasted death.[43]

In contrast to Moltmann, for whom God's *suffering* is the distinctively Christian mode of thinking about God, Gavrilyuk with Cyril recognizes that it is the *redemption* of suffering that is the crowning achievement of Christian thought. Salvation is once again the litmus test.

Moltmann, and those who follow in his vein, propose a suffering God in the face of the extent of suffering in the world. The suffering of God in eternity is sometimes proposed as a response to the problem of evil. There is suffering all around us, but God suffers too. However, as Gavrilyuk notes, 'Far from offering a compelling theodicy, the projection of humanity's suffering onto the inner life of God only compounds the problem of evil'.[44] The consequences of proposing a God who experiences suffering in eternity can be to rob him of his power to save. Thomas Weinandy puts this best: 'Ironically, those who advocate a suffering God, having locked suffering within God's divine nature, have actually locked God out of human suffering.'[45]

The central question here is whether, from the point of view of salvation, God undergoing suffering in order to understand or empathize with the suffering of his creatures is sufficient to redeem us from such suffering. And, further, whether God's inability to suffer can be given up so lightly without consequences for how we understand our salvation to be achieved.

To suggest that God simply understands our suffering is an insufficient response in the face of that suffering. From our own experience of pain and suffering, we can understand the pain and suffering even of those to whom we are causing pain and suffering. Our understanding does not necessarily do anything to prevent or redeem their suffering. Moreover, suffering with those who suffer may offer little redemption from the suffering of those who suffer. We might voluntarily decide to share in the sufferings of a particular group of people by being beaten with them, but our suffering does not lessen theirs. As Richard Bauckham notes: 'It is no consolation to the sufferer to know that God is as much a helpless victim of evil as he is himself.'[46]

It is in this light that we can turn to Dietrich Bonhoeffer's famous phrase quoted at the beginning of this chapter: 'only a suffering God can help'.[47] This phrase tends to be interpreted as an argument for divine passibility. God *must* suffer, and therefore be able to suffer, in order to redeem: 'only a *suffering* God can help'. Bonhoeffer, or at least these words of Bonhoeffer, are brought as evidence in favour of God's passibility by those who wish to argue God's ability to suffer and change.

However, such an approach misreads the thrust of Bonhoeffer's claim, that 'only a suffering *God* can help'. It is not the suffering in itself that is redemptive, it is the one who has taken that suffering to himself. Writing on another attribute of God, Bonhoeffer writes: 'Love is not what He *does* and what He *suffers,* but it is what *He* does and what *He* suffers'.[48] It is the fact that it is *God* who suffers in Christ which enables the suffering to be redemptive, as even the suffering of a sinless human being would be of no help. In the words of the philosopher Martin Heidegger, 'only a God can save us'.[49]

It is crucial for our salvation that it is God who redeems us, who suffers for us. Here is where the affirmation of divine impassibility becomes important. It is precisely because God is unable to suffer, because he is God, that God's 'suffering' redeems suffering. Unlike any created agent to whom suffering is something inflicted upon them, God's 'suffering' changes the nature of suffering because it is unable to be inflicted upon him. His impassibility prevents suffering from having the final word. Weinandy underlines this point:

> It is only because the persons of the Trinity reside in an ontological order distinct from that of the created order, and so are not contaminated with the malady of evil, that they, in their immutably all-consuming and perfect love, are able to so act in time and history as to unite us to themselves, thus freeing us from the wages of sin and rescuing us from the ravages of death.[50]

We need to unpack Bonhoeffer's famous phrase a little more here. In context, Bonhoeffer's statement is a wider one on human religiosity and doing away 'with a false conception of God'.[51] Human religiosity experiences distress and looks to a mighty saviour to intervene as a 'deus ex machina' – a superhero who appears from nowhere to bring an end to such distress. The difference between Christianity and human religiosity, Bonhoeffer argues, is that Christianity doesn't posit a saviour who delivers us with a powerful overcoming *of* suffering but *through* it. God in Christ is not a mighty superhero, but an innocent seemingly powerless in the face of torture and execution. In a subsequent letter Bonhoeffer reiterates that this 'is a reversal of what the religious man expects from God'.[52]

It is in this context that Bonhoeffer ascribes suffering to God, often with the important qualification 'in the world' or 'in Christ': 'God lets himself be pushed out of the world onto the cross. He is weak and powerless *in the world*, and that is precisely the way, the only way, in which he is with us and helps us.'[53] Our response to this, according to Bonhoeffer, is to be 'caught up in the messianic sufferings of God in Jesus Christ'.[54] In so doing, 'we throw ourselves completely into the arms of God, taking seriously, not our own sufferings, but those of God in the world'.[55]

Caution is needed. There is a danger that we could misread Bonhoeffer here as advocating a seeking out of suffering. From the earliest days of Christianity there have been those who have actively sought suffering and martyrdom to get close to God. The most famous example of this is probably the second-century martyr Ignatius of Antioch, who pleaded with his readers to 'allow me to become food for the wild beasts, through whose instrumentality it will be granted me to attain to God'.[56] Suffering as a result of following God's will and entering into situations that will inevitably lead to suffering is one thing. Seeking suffering for its own sake is another. There is quite enough suffering the world, and suffering may well result from seeking God, without needing to seek suffering *in order to* become close to God. Moreover, we risk identifying God *only* with suffering. Bonhoeffer also insists that

> God must be recognized at the centre of life, not just when we are at the end of our resources; he wills to be recognized in life, and not just when death comes; in health and vigour, and not just in our suffering; in our activities and not just in sin.[57]

More crucially, however, we need to explore the nature of God's sufferings in the world. God's sufferings are not a special class of suffering different from ours, which we might be tempted to think if we read Bonhoeffer too quickly. Rather, the sufferings of God in Christ are not separate from our suffering. They are our suffering. Proponents of a passible God, who suggest that God suffers himself or even that when we suffer God suffers too, empty the mystery of God suffering in Christ of its redemptive power. It is precisely *our* suffering that God takes to himself in Christ in order to transform it. There is no additional suffering in him that brings about redemption, but the transformation of *our* suffering in him.

Williams puts this best, in a passage that's worth quoting at length:

> It is not that we must 'make' the Word suffer in its divinity in order for the Word to be credible to human suffering: the suffering that the Word takes to itself in the Incarnation is the absolutely specific human pain of Jesus and, consequently, the specific pain of all those for whom the Word in Jesus speaks. It is not an unimaginable 'divine' suffering but yours and mine in their historic particularity. And it is not that the divine Son by some supreme act of identification 'feels' our pain as if it were his own, but rather that the divine agency inhabits completely the pain that is ours and gives it voice precisely as *human* pain and as *our* pain.[58]

God takes *our* suffering to himself in Christ. He does not leave us to suffer. He becomes one of us and takes our suffering to himself in Christ. He is therefore, in Gavrilyuk's words, 'neither eternally indifferent to suffering, nor eternally overwhelmed by it'.[59] St Gregory of Nyssa (c. 330–c. 395 CE) notes that just as a doctor heals without needing to acquire the sickness of his patient, so when God transforms our suffering, 'the suffering does not touch him, it is he who touches the disease'.[60]

This is a key insight for those attempting to build a pattern for Christian action from the classical Christian doctrine of God. God does not just suffer sympathetically *with* us, nor just in order to understand our suffering empathetically in solidarity with us. Rather, God transforms our suffering *for* us. The suffering of God in Christ is the intentional redemption of suffering humanity by the impassible God *for* our salvation.

God's transformation of human suffering alerts us to the need to play our part in the transformation of earthly suffering. Where we encounter suffering and pain we are called to play our part in alleviating them. The suffering of the impassible God, his transformation of suffering, alerts us to the fact that suffering is not merely to be tolerated as a fact of creaturely existence but to be confronted in all its forms. Where it is in our capacity to alleviate the suffering of others, God's transformation of suffering alerts us to the Christian calling to alleviate pain and suffering so far as we are able. Sometimes we can work to bring about an end of the situation which is causing suffering and pain. For those whose pain and suffering may be permanent or life-long we can accompany them, and journey with them in Christian solidarity so that at least we overcome the pain of suffering alone. As God took our suffering to himself in Christ, so through our ministry and pastoral care we share with those whose suffering may be life-ending or life-long.

However, caution is needed here that we do not equate Christian action simply with activism or with ministries that transform or come alongside suffering individuals and painful situations. In Christ, God not only transforms suffering through what he *does* but by what he undergoes. Sometimes it is only the absence of agency, or by the withdrawal of it, that transformation is brought about and a transforming mirror is held to the realities of our human ways of doing and being.[61] Christ's passion is transformative as much for what he does to death as for what he reveals about the systems of human power and religiosity in allowing himself to be taken into the hands of his betrayers. The one who waits and endures can transform a situation as much as the one who organizes and overcomes. Both are needed in order to realize the transformation of those instances of suffering caused by systems and structures of human injustice. The patient sitting of the Rosa Parks of this world is as vital to such transformation as the organizing activity of the Martin Luther Kings.

In Christ, the very limits of suffering, even death itself, have been destroyed by God. *Our* suffering, *our* death has been destroyed. We know this as witnesses to the Resurrection. God doesn't suffer suffering. He transforms it. And he asks us to do likewise, to transform and put an end to all the suffering we see – except that as human beings we're often more likely to be the cause of suffering than the cure of it. God's suffering transforms *our* suffering and means that he, not that suffering, is the last Word.

As human beings we cling to power; God sheds it. As human beings we flee suffering; God transforms it. As human beings we cause suffering; God endures it. Christ is his last word on the matter. God suffers with us, but more importantly, *for us* – so that in that last word we too might be fully alive in him.

Notes

1 Bonhoeffer, D., *Letters and Papers from Prison* (London: SCM Press, 2001), p. 134.

2 Surin, K., 'The Impassibility of God and the Problem of Evil', in the *Scottish Journal of Theology* 35 (1982), pp. 97–115, 105; cited in Bauckham, R., 'Only the Suffering God Can Help – Divine Passibility in Modern Theology', in *Themelios* 9.3 (April 1984), pp. 6–12, 12. Moltmann also makes reference to Auschwitz: 'Even Auschwitz is in God himself... God in Auschwitz and Auschwitz in the crucified God', *The Crucified God* (London: SCM Press, 1974), p. 278.

3 Moltmann, J., *Crucified*, p. 1.

4 Gavrilyuk, P., 'God's Impassible Suffering in the Flesh: The Promise of Paradoxical Christology', in White, T. J. and Keating, J. (eds), *Divine Impassibility and the Mystery of Human Suffering* (Grand Rapids, MI: Eerdmans, 2009), pp. 127–49, 138.

5 Gavrilyuk, 'Suffering in the Flesh', p. 138.

6 Gavrilyuk, 'Suffering in the Flesh', p. 138.

7 Moltmann, J., 'Jürgen Moltmann', in Moltmann, J. (ed.), *How I Have Changed: Reflections on Thirty Years of Theology* (London: SCM Press, 1997), p. 18; cf. Moltmann, J., *Experiences in Theology: Ways and Forms of Christian Theology* (Minneapolis: Fortress Press, 2000), pp. 304–5.

8 See above for our discussion of the unity of the Trinity that divine simplicity protects (pp. 28–30).

9 Moltmann, *Experiences*, p. 305; see also Moltmann, *Crucified*, p. 151: 'The abandonment on the cross which separates the Son from the Father is something which takes place within God himself; it is stasis within God – "God against God" ... We must not allow ourselves to overlook this "enmity" between God and God by failing to take seriously either the rejection of Jesus by God ... or his last cry to God upon the cross.'

10 Cyril of Jerusalem, *Catechetical Lectures* 4.7.

11 Moltmann, *Crucified*, p. 4.

12 To see Christ as abandoned by God at his crucifixion renders especially problematic an article of the creed which is perhaps the most overlooked in contemporary theology. This is the 'descent into hell' referred to in 1 Peter 3.18–20. The divine identity of the Christ who descends into hell is essential for the redemptive exchange that occurs (see Chrysostom's Paschal Homily below). The descent into hell is experiencing something of a resurgence in the wake of the importance given to it in von Balthasar, H., *Mysterium Paschale*, (San Francisco: Ignatius Press, 2000). See Emerson, M. Y., *He Descended to the Dead: An Evangelical Theology of Holy Saturday* (Downers Grove, IL: Inter-Varsity Press, 2019); Pitstick, L., *Christ's Descent into Hell: John Paul II, Joseph Ratzinger, and Hans Urs von Balthasar on the Theology of Holy Saturday* (Grand Rapids, MI: Eerdmans, 2016). Given George Steiner's observation that all of our earthly journey is that of Holy Saturday, theological reflection on Holy Saturday and the credal 'descent into hell' is especially important (see Steiner, G., *Real Presences* (Chicago: University of Chicago Press, 1989)).

13 Moltmann, J., *The Trinity and the Kingdom of God* (London: SCM Press, 1981), p. 21.

14 Moltmann often distinguishes between monotheism and Trinitarianism in such a way as to suggest that Trinitarianism implies a kind of tritheism and doesn't also entail the fundamental unity of God while also mysteriously recognizing the threeness of the persons God has revealed himself to be. For example, the divine suffering of love outwards is grounded on the pain of love within... We can only talk about God's suffering in Trinitarian terms. In monotheism it is impossible' (Moltmann, *Trinity*, p. 25).

15 Moltmann, J., *The Future of Creation* (Minneapolis: Fortress Press 2007), p. 93. Elsewhere Moltmann sees change as an essential feature of Trinitarian thought, further departing from the eternal Trinitarian relationship of Christian orthodoxy: 'Anyone who denies movement in the divine nature also denies the divine Trinity. And to deny this is really to deny the whole Christian faith.' (Moltmann, *Trinity*, p. 45). Affirming the God of classical theism is not to affirm a static monad, but that the relationship between Father, Son and Holy Spirit are eternal and not subject to change. Suggesting that change is a feature of the Trinitarian God runs dangerously close to modalism, the heresy which states that Father, Son and Holy Spirit are different stages in the history of the Godhead, each referring to a different 'mode' in the life of the Trinity rather than eternal 'persons'. Whereas Arianism and tritheism overemphasize the distinction between the persons, modalism overemphasizes the nature of their oneness.

16 Cf. Durham, *Word Biblical Commentary, Exodus,* p. 39 on Exod. 3.14.

17 Moltmann, *Trinity,* p. 54.

18 Moltmann, *Crucified,* p. 246.

19 Moltmann, *Crucified,* pp. 227–8.

20 Moltmann, J., *The Church in the Power of the Spirit* (Minneapolis: Fortress Press, 1993), p. 113; cf. Moltman, *Trinity,* p. 22.

21 Cf. Moltmann, *Trinity,* p. 54: 'Can God really be content to be sufficient for himself if he *is* love?' The perfect relationship between Father, Son and Holy Spirit is sufficient to hold that the nature of God's love exceeds a lonely isolationism on the one hand, and prevents the existence of creation as a necessary object for God to love. The love between Father, Son and Holy Spirit means that God is love *and* that his love for his creation (and therefore us) is not necessary but sheer gift. He does not need the world to be love. Moltmann is entirely wrong in saying that 'God 'needs' the world and man. If God is love, then he neither will be nor can be without the one who is his beloved' (*Trinity,* p. 58). It is because God is love that he loves us, not because he needs us in order to be loved.

22 Moltmann muddies, if not obliterates, the distinction between Creator and creation that we traced in the previous chapter. Instead of classical theism's insistence that God differs fundamentally from creation because he exists 'outside' it as creator, Moltmann entwines creation with creator: 'Creation is part of the eternal love affair between the Father and the Son. It springs from the Father's love for the Son and is redeemed by the answering love of the Son for the Father' (*Trinity,* p. 59).

23 Moltmann, *Trinity,* p. 22; see also Moltmann, *Crucified,* p. 214: 'Christian theology has adopted this concept of God from philosophical theology down to the present day.'

24 Gavrilyuk, P., *The Suffering of the Impassible God* (Oxford: Oxford University Press, 2004), p. 2. In an appendix he lists examples of many scholarly instances of the claim that divine impassibility is a philosophical perversion (Gavrilyuk, *Impassible,* pp. 176–9).

25 Gavrilyuk, *Impassible,* p. 3.

26 Gavrilyuk, *Impassible,* p. 51.

27 For a good summary of the biblical basis of classical theism, especially divine simplicity, see Dolezal, *All That Is In God,* pp. 37–58.

28 These verses are applied to establish the eternity of the Son by the author of the letter to the Hebrews (Heb. 1.10–12). See also Ps. 90.2.

29 There is some debate as to whether עוֹלָם *(olam)* conveys the idea of timeless eternity or an eternity of full duration of the ages. See especially Kim, E., 'Biblical Understandings of Time', in *Time, Eternity and the Trinity: A Trinitarian Analogical Understanding of Time and Eternity*

(Eugene, OR: Pickwick Publications, 2010), pp. 17–60; Craig, W. L., *Time and Eternity: Exploring God's Relationship to Time* (Wheaton, IL: Crossway, 2001). Though dated, Rust, E., 'Time and Eternity in Biblical Thought', in *Theology Today* 10.3 (1953), pp. 327–56, remains helpful.

30 Hengel, M., *Judaism and Hellenism: Studies in Their Encounter in Palestine During the Early Hellenistic Period* (London: SCM Press, 1974).

31 Gavrilyuk, *Impassible*, p. 15.

32 Gavrilyuk, *Impassible*, p. 15.

33 Gavrilyuk, *Impassible*, p. 49; cf. Gavrilyuk, 'Suffering in the Flesh', p. 139.

34 Jenson. R., 'Ipse Pater Non Est Impassibilis', in White, T. J. and Keating, J. (eds), *Divine Impassibility and the Mystery of Suffering* (Grand Rapids, MI: Eerdmans, 2009), pp. 117–26, 124. For an introduction to Jenson's theology, see Harvey, L., *Jesus in the Trinity: A Beginner's Guide to the Theology of Robert Jenson* (London: SCM Press, 2020).

35 Gavrilyuk, *Impassible*, p. 61.

36 Bauckham, 'Only the Suffering', p. 9.

37 St John Chrysostom, *Paschal Homily*, available at http://anglicansonline.org/special/Easter/chrysostom_easter.html (accessed 15.8.19).

38 Whitehead, A. N., *Process and Reality* (New York: Free Press, 1978), p. 351.

39 Gavrilyuk, *Impassible*, p. 174.

40 Gavrilyuk, *Impassible*, p. 174.

41 On the debate between Cyril and Nestorius see Williams, *Heart of Creation*, pp. 66–8.

42 Cyril of Alexandria, *Third Letter to Nestorius* 12; available at: https://www.uniontheology.org/resources/doctrine/jesus/third-letter-to-nestorius (accessed 13.8.19).

43 Cyril of Alexandria, *Second Letter to Nestorius*; available at https://www.uniontheology.org/resources/doctrine/jesus/second-letter-to-nestorius (accessed 13.8.19).

44 Gavrilyuk, *Impassible*, p. 145.

45 Weinandy, T., 'Does God Suffer?', in *Ars Disputandi* 2 (2002), pp. 1–13; cited in Gavrilyuk, *Impassible*, p. 147.

46 Bauckham, 'Only the Suffering', p. 12.

47 Bonhoeffer, *Letters*, p. 134. I'm indebted to Mark Knight for most of the thoughts on Bonhoeffer that follow.

48 Bonhoeffer, D., *Ethics* (New York: Macmillan, 1950), p. 174, cited in Yee, J. L., *God Suffers For Us: A Systematic Inquiry into a Concept of Divine Passibility* (The Hague: Martinus Nijhoff, 1974), pp. 7–8.

49 Heidegger, M., 'Nur noch ein Gott kann uns retten', in *Der Spiegel* 30 (May 1976), pp. 193–219; (trans. Richardson, W.), 'Only a God Can Save Us', in Sheehan, T. (ed.), *Heidegger: The Man*, pp. 45–67; available at: www.ditext.com/heidegger/interview.html (accessed 25.8.19). The difference between Heidegger's God and Bonhoeffer's is one of presence. Bonhoeffer's God is present but pushed to the margins in the suffering of the world and given the appearance of his absence. Heidegger's God is absent. Bonhoeffer calls us to participate with God's sufferings in the world. Heidegger calls us to a posture of readiness for his arrival, or a readying of readiness in others. However, this readiness involves recognizing that ultimate control lies beyond us and that we cannot ultimately invoke a God to do *our* will.

50 Weinandy, T., 'God and Human Suffering', in White, T. J. and Keating, J. (eds), *Divine Impassibility and the Mystery of Suffering* (Cambridge: Eerdmans, 2009), pp. 99–116, 115–16.

51 Bonhoeffer, *Letters*, p. 134.

52 Bonhoeffer, *Letters*, p. 135.

53 Bonhoeffer, *Letters*, p. 134. Emphasis mine.

54 Bonhoeffer, *Letters*, p. 135.

55 Bonhoeffer, *Letters*, p. 134.

56 *Epistle to the Romans* 4; available at www.newadvent.org/fathers/0107.htm (accessed 17.8.19).

57 Bonhoeffer, *Letters*, p. 111.

58 Williams, *Heart of Creation*, p. 92. See also pp. 203–17 for a discussion of Bonhoeffer's concept of *Stellvertretung* ('vicarious representative action') which related to Christ's suffering and an ethics that derives from that.

59 Gavrilyuk, *Impassible*, p. 149.

60 Gregory of Nyssa, *Against Eunomius* 6.3; available at: www.ccel.org/ccel/schaff/npnf205.viii.i.viii.iii.html (accessed 13.8.19); cited at Gavrilyuk, *Impassible*, p. 9.

61 Vanstone, W. H., *The Stature of Waiting* (London: Dartman, Longman & Todd, 2004) offers the best account of this insight.

3

The Love of God

'How soon is it said, Love is God! This also is short: if you count it, it is one: if you weigh it, how great is it! Love is God, and he that dwells, says he, in love, dwells in God, and God dwells in him. Let God be your house, and be a house of God; dwell in God, and let God dwell in you. God dwells in you, that He may hold you: you dwell in God, that you may not fall; for thus says the apostle of this same charity, Charity never falls. How should He fall whom God holds?' (St Augustine)[1]

Tina Turner famously sang: 'What's love got to do, got to do with it? What's love but a second hand emotion?' In short, the Christian answer to her question is: 'Everything'.

In this chapter we will explore the nature of God's love, what it means for God to *be* love and, crucially, what it means for us to put love into action. This chapter will be the first that deals especially with what it means for us to act in a way that is inspired by the God of classical theism. In what follows, we begin to explore what Christian action might look like if it is inspired by the Christian doctrine of God.

In the last chapter we explored why it is important for our salvation that God is incapable of suffering, and how he transforms *our* suffering by his inability to suffer. In this chapter we deal with what it means to say that God *is* love.

Before we spell out what it means for God to love, there is one more aspect of the argument for the suffering God that is relevant to his love. One of the arguments used by those who

support the notion that God suffers is that suffering is a necessary part of loving. Once again, Moltmann offers us the classic
expression of such a view: 'if God were incapable of suffering
in every respect, then he would also be incapable of love'.[2]

It may be that loving in the world necessarily requires
suffering. In a sinful world, where human beings selfishly cling
to what is their own and genuine fear of loss prevents complete
self-gift, love often entails the pain of an unheeded or abused
gift. Our experience of love is often that of incomplete com-
promise and rejection. Herbert McCabe best describes the
curious human relationship to love:

> We cannot live without love and yet we are afraid of the
> destructive creative power of love. We need and deeply want
> to be loved and to love, and yet when that happens it seems a
> threat, because we are asked to give ourselves up, to abandon
> our selves; and so when we meet love we kill it.[3]

Moreover, McCabe reminds us that it is precisely because of
the totality of God's love for us in Christ that he is rejected:
'If you love enough you will be killed. Humankind inevitably
rejects the only solution to its problem, the solution of love.'[4]

However, Moltmann goes further than this. He suggests that
love involves suffering *in eternity*:

> the suffering of love does not only affect the redeeming acts
> of God outwards; it also affects the trinitarian fellowship in
> God himself. In this way the extra-trinitarian suffering and
> the inner-trinitarian suffering correspond. For the divine
> suffering of love outwards is grounded on the pain of love
> within.[5]

Moltmann seems to think that all love requires suffering.
He argues that 'in order to be completely itself, love has to
suffer. It suffers from whatever contradicts its own nature.'[6]
He anticipates the objection that there is nothing contrary to
God in God: 'But if God is love and nothing but love, can

there be anything that contradicts his being, so that he suffers from it and has to endure it as part of his own self-sacrifice? What is this? It is evil ... By suffering evil he transforms evil into good.'[7] Once again, Moltmann restricts the freedom of God by making creation necessary for the completion of God. The consequences of this are profound. No longer is it the case that God is love without qualification. No longer is creation a completely free gift; rather it seems that God requires creation to fulfil his potential to love.

Moltmann's argument here is based on the necessity of suffering for love to be love: 'The one who is capable of love is also capable of suffering, for he also opens himself to the suffering which is involved in love, and yet remains superior to it by virtue of his love.'[8] However, Moltmann makes little argument for why suffering is necessary for love, even if suffering may be a necessary consequence of love *within* creation. In eternity, where God exists in and as perfect love, there is none of the fear and rejection which give rise to the suffering of love in the created order. As we read in 1 John 4.18: 'There is no fear in love, but perfect love casts out fear.' As we shall see, the perfect love of Father, Son and Holy Spirit is not so much about the necessity of suffering as the perfect freedom of self-emptying gift.

What gives rise to Moltmann's equation of love and suffering? We have seen repeatedly that the distinction between creature and Creator is at the heart of affirming the God of classical theism. Gavrilyuk notes how the affirmation of the simplicity of God and the unity of his attributes is a guard against idolatry:

> The omnipotence of God cannot be separated from his perfect goodness, for in God all attributes are united in a union beyond description. There can be no better panacea from all forms of human idolatry, power grabbing, and tyranny than the overflowing goodness and the self-emptying love of the omnipotent God.[9]

Those who ascribe suffering to God in the manner we traced in our previous chapter tend to describe God in terms which present a God in our creaturely image. McCabe notes this particularly strongly: 'The idea of God suffering in sympathy with creation represents a regrettable regression from the traditional insistence on the mystery of God and can be seen as a kind of idolatry'.[10]

Moltmann's equation of suffering with love is one example of the tendency to describe divine attributes with reference to human ones, rather than seek to model creaturely human attributes on their divine counterpart, as far as we are able within our creaturely limits. The argument of this book, which we shall see particularly in relation to God's anger in the next chapter, is that modelling our action on God's attributes is a fruitful ground for Christian action. This is especially so in the light of the identity of divine attributes suggested by divine simplicity, which illuminates what initially appear to us as contradictory divine attributes.

Approaches such as Moltmann's run the risk of making our human experience the basis of our understanding of God's love. Such approaches discover a concept of love by observing the inevitable suffering involved in loving within the created order, and then apply that concept to what it means for God to love. This approach is just one example of the tendency to project creaturely limits onto the Creator. There are other forms of this tendency too. For example, modelling divine love on other forms of human love such as romantic or passionate love, and suggesting that God's love is similar to our romantic or passionate forms of loving.

As human beings, we are always ready to make God in our own image. We mistake God's love for an image of human love, and we shape God's love in our image. As Christians, we know that our vocation is instead to be shaped into God's image – to reclaim that image given to us in creation and that likeness renewed in our baptism. We know that our images of God are to be shaped by him, not made by us and our creaturely projections of what it means to love.

Except that, as human beings, we're pretty useless at loving. We can make the mistake of thinking we know what love is – complete with the hearts and flowers and cards that the world around us tells us love is – and we make God into a kind of romantic superhero. As Brian Davies notes: 'If to love means to be moved by passion as we can sometimes be when we love, then I should certainly agree that God cannot love. We will not understand the love of God by taking as our paradigm the case of the romantic love.'[11]

Alternatively, we can project other images onto God in order to try to understand what it means for God to be love. We can reduce God's love to a kind of banal niceness. God becomes a sort of constant friend who supports us, but never challenges us to step outside of our comfort zones or the lives we've made for ourselves. God becomes a sort of comfortable blanket that keeps us warm. Or, more painfully, we project our experience of love onto God. The failings of those who were supposed to teach us what it means to love get projected onto God, and we find it difficult to believe that he loves us at all. Our painful experience of love means it is difficult for us to work out what God's love might be.

How are we to avoid such projections? How are we to conceive of God's love in a way that allows that very love to transform us and the world around us?

One possible approach is negative or apophatic. As St Paul demonstrates in his first letter to the Corinthians, it is rather easier to say what love is not: 'Love is not envious or boastful or arrogant or rude. It does not insist on its own way; it is not irritable or resentful; it does not rejoice in wrongdoing, but rejoices in the truth' (1 Cor. 13.4–7).

However, we can go further. We know that if we want to know anything about God's love, our starting point is Christ. If we want to know what love is, we look to Christ. The author of the first letter of John reminds us that in Christ God showed us what it means for him to be love: 'God's love was revealed among us in this way: God sent his only Son into the world so that we might live through him' (1 John 4.9). Likewise, St Paul in his letter to the Romans taught us that 'God proves his love for us in that while we still were sinners Christ died for us' (Rom. 5.8). In the life and death of Christ, God's love is revealed.

Christ stands as the ultimate refuter of our images of what God might be like. Christ is the communication of God's very self to us in our humanity itself. If we fall foul of the temptation to make God in our own image, Christ ever stands against it. This is never more the case than when we come to think of God's love. What do these events – the Incarnation and the Crucifixion – reveal about the nature of God's love?

Both the Incarnation and the Crucifixion reveal to us that God's love is complete self-gift. The Incarnation is the mystery of God's birth as a human being in Christ. He becomes one of us for our salvation. The Incarnation is the mystery of God's gift of himself to us. The Crucifixion is the mystery of God's undergoing suffering and death for us in Christ to transform our suffering and death. If the Incarnation underlines the nature of God's love as gift, the Crucifixion reminds us of the extent of that gift. The life of Christ as God's gift of himself is total even to the point of death: 'no one has greater love than this, to lay down one's life for one's friends' (John 15.3).

Moreover, the Incarnation and the Crucifixion cannot be separated. The birth of Jesus Christ is the birth of God as one of us (as the previous chapter recognized that St Cyril of Alexandria saw so clearly). The death of Jesus Christ is not the innocent death of a sinless man, but the death of God as one of us. The death of Jesus Christ is the death of God's human way of being, so that our way of being might be completely transformed by the redemptive love of God. In his life, death, and resurrection, Christ shows us God's love.

Christ shows us what it means to be God within the limits of our creaturely understanding. God remains transcendent to those creaturely limits, even as he lives as one of us. This is the theme of numerous Christmas sermons which reflect on the mystery of the Creator of the Universe becoming one of us within in his creation. For just one example we can turn to St Augustine, who is worth quoting at length:

> Christ, the only-begotten Son of God, the true Sun of Justice, so shone upon the earth as not to leave the heavens, remaining there eternally, but coming hither for a time; there determining the everlasting day, here enduring the day of humanity; there living perpetually without the passage of time, here dying in time without the inroads of sin; there remaining in life without end, here freeing our life from the destruction of death ... here suffering evil; there never dying, here rising after death and bestowing eternal life on mortals. God became man so that man might become God. The Lord took the form of a servant so that man might be turned to God. The Founder and Inhabitant of heaven dwelt upon earth so that man might rise from earth to heaven.[12]

If Christ shows us something of what it means to be God within the limits of creaturely understanding, he also sets forth within our creaturely understanding what it means to be human. Jane Williams notes the shock that we might feel at realizing that the Incarnation is not about God becoming like us, but rather about ourselves as human beings becoming like him: 'Sad, egocentric, embittered, and self-obsessed as we are, we have tended to assume that Jesus became human like us, but now, illuminatingly, we discover that we are invited to become human like him.'[13] Christ reveals to us the nature of God's love, and in doing so he sets forth how we are called to be human, if we are to be the humans that God is calling us to be. So, we see why love is the heart of the Christian faith. In God's love, the central tenets of the Christian faith all come together. God as love, ultimate self-gift, reveals to us the Trinity – God's very self – the eternal gift of Father completely to Son completely to Holy Spirit; Incarnation – God's eternal gift of himself in us; and Sacrament – God's gift of himself to us in the sacraments of the Church until the end of time.

All of these, the Trinity, the Incarnation, the sacramental system, are revealed to us in 1 John 4.9: 'God sent his only *Son* into the world that we might live through him.' The Trinity reveals to us that God's love for us is totally unnecessary, because creation is totally unnecessary. God does not need us as something with which to relate, or as a means of suffering to perfect his love. Creation is entirely unnecessary and because it's unnecessary, it is entirely gift. This is the Christian meaning of Grace. God doesn't need us to be love. God's love is perfect in itself. We know this from the doctrine of the Trinity – Father, Son, and Holy Spirit. God doesn't create us as a playmate or because he is lonely. He exists as perfect love. Father poured out to Son poured out to Spirit and vice versa. God exists in eternity as perfect, self-emptying love. He creates us extravagantly as sheer gift.

Likewise, the Incarnation reveals to us what God's love means for us. 'God *sent* his only Son *into the world* so that we might live through him.' God's love isn't something that happens at a distance. God's love for us means that he sends his only Son. God's love for us means he became one of us and took humanity to himself. God's love is not static or self-interested. The Incarnation as the keystone of classical theism is the ultimate proof against the supposed Christian adoption of the disinterested God of the philosophers. The Incarnation as a, if not *the*, central feature of classical theism reminds us that God does not cling to himself. God's love does not cling to itself. The Incarnation also reminds us that God's love is not earned. We're not loved by God because we love God. We love God because we are loved by him, and in creating us and becoming one of us, he made us and he made us able to love. In Christ, he showed us what it is to love. We love because he is love (1 John 4.19).

The sacraments, God's gift of his life among us in his Body and in his Church, remind us that the ascension of Christ is not the end of God's love for us. 'God sent his only Son into the world so that *we might live through him.*' God's love for us is complete in Christ, but it doesn't end in the year 33 CE. The Resurrection teaches us that God's love never ends. Not even death can get in its way. God may have revealed his love to us completely in Christ, but he doesn't ever stop the self-emptying that is at the centre of the mystery of the Trinity, that is the ground for the Incarnation, and that is the foundation of the sacraments. God pours himself out in Christ. God pours himself out in the presence of his Spirit in the Church, and no more so than in the sacraments of his Church. The sacraments are the best means we have of receiving God's gift of himself, the guaranteed meeting places in creation of his love poured out. The sacramental life – the regular, lively, and life-giving celebration and reception of the sacraments – is a life soaked in God's gift of himself – a life founded on God's love.

If we want to know what God's love is like, we look to Christ's life – the whole of that life. The Crucifixion is an inseparable part of that incarnate life. The Cross is not the scene of God's abandonment of Christ, but the consequence of God's self-emptying love to the very end. The Cross is the result of the meeting place of love and the rest of humanity that inevitably rejects that love, as McCabe reminds us: 'Humankind inevitably rejects the only solution to its problem, the solution of love. Human history rejects its own meaning. Humankind is doomed.'[14]

The Cross gives us the best image we have of God's love. This is the image of how that life seemed, at first, to come to an end. The Cross shows us what it means to love. Or, rather, it makes explicit the extent of God's love for us, the lengths to which he will go for us and the consequences of what it means to love. In Christ we see God's love poured out at each and every moment, not just in his death but in the whole of his life. It is his death that stands as the ultimate sign of where loving will take you: 'if you love enough you will be killed'.[15]

The irony is rich here. The humanity that rejects the love of God to the point of death is the very same humanity that in that death is restored to life. God's love is poured out so completely that it is the means of redemption for the humanity that so utterly rejects it. Christ in his life and death reveals to us that God's love is the perfect and eternal gift of self-giving and self-emptying. This is the love which is revealed to us in the Trinity, the perfect gift of self-emptying to each other in love. This self-emptying turns out to be what God's love is after all, what love is after all.

Now we see why it's easier to say what love is not than what love is. Love is a kind of self-negation, not a denial of self but an emptying of self. Love is the pouring out of one's self for the other in love.

Again, caution is needed here. The perfect image of love we encounter on the Cross doesn't call us to a morbid emulation – we're not called to *seek out* pain and misery in order to repeat the Crucifixion. We're not called to aimless self-abasement. Loving *may* entail suffering and will very likely take us into situations where suffering is more or less guaranteed, because, as McCabe noted, when human beings 'meet love we kill it'.[16]

In fact, to pour ourselves out fully we need to be fully aware of the self we are called to be and called to pour out. The trinitarian love of Father, Son and Holy Spirit involves the fullness of those persons being poured out fully for each other in love. In order for the Son to know the Father, the Father must know himself first.

The kind of self-emptying that is revealed as God's love calls us to lay aside the false self we've created for ourselves and all those images and idols to which we cling. Here in this self-negation we encounter the mystery of God, because as we lay aside that self, as we pour that self out, as we love, we find that we are actually more really ourselves than we were at the outset.

'Those who find their life will lose it, and those who lose their life for my sake will find it' (Matt. 10.39). We lose ourselves only to find ourself. We lay aside our life only to take up the life that God is offering to us even today. We pour ourselves out and find ourselves swept up in that eternal self-offering which is the life of God himself, God's love.

In the last chapter we suggested that a key insight for those attempting to build a pattern for Christian action from the classical Christian doctrine of God was that God transforms our suffering *for* us. The suffering he takes to himself is not incidental but intentional, in order to redeem human suffering from the inside. In considering the nature of God's love we discover another key insight for Christian action. Not only should Christian action be intentional, but it involves the whole of our selves. To love as God loves is to pour ourselves out completely for the other, not needlessly but intentionally.

All of this may sound a little too easy. 'Be intentional, be self-aware as you give it your all.' The difficulty of living the Christian life cannot be reduced to an easy catchphrase of how to live.[17] Unfortunately, McCabe is right. Humankind *is* doomed. But, crucially, we know that God loves us, and we know that God *is* love. Moreover, we know that Christ came to share in humanity's self-damnation. Bonhoeffer describes this process: 'God lets himself be pushed out of the world on to the cross.'[18] Humanity rejects the very love that would save it. And yet because that was rejection of the impassible, eternal, loving God, it could never ultimately succeed. The love of God encounters the rejection and suffering caused by humankind, and transforms humanity even in that act of rejection and suffering, raising us to new life in him.

In this, above all else, God shows his love for us. Humankind is loved, and humankind is called to love – a little less like the images of love we make for ourselves, and a little more like the image of God in which all of us have been made.

Notes

1 Augustine, *Homily* 9.1; available at: www.newadvent.org/fathers/170209.htm (accessed 19.8.19).

2 Moltmann, *The Trinity and the Kingdom of God*, p. 22.

3 McCabe, H., *God Matters* (London: Continuum, 2010), p. 95.

4 McCabe, *God Matters*, p. 124.

5 Moltmann, *Trinity*, pp. 24–5; see also, Moltmann, *The Crucified God*, p. 230: 'There are other forms of suffering between unwilling suffering as a result of an alien cause and being essentially unable to suffer, namely active suffering, the suffering of love, in which one voluntarily opens himself to the possibility of being affected by another. There is unwilling suffering, there is accepted suffering, and there is the suffering of love.'

6 Moltmann, *Trinity*, p. 33.

7 Moltmann, *Trinity*, p. 33.

8 Moltmann, *Crucified*, p. 230.

9 Gavrilyuk, 'God's Impassible Suffering in the Flesh', p. 137.

10 McCabe, *God Matters*, p. 1.

11 Davies, B., 'Classical Theism and the Doctrine of Divine Simplicity', in Davies, B. (ed.), *Language, Meaning and God: Essays in Honor of Herbert McCabe* (Eugene, OR: Wipf and Stock, 2010), pp. 51–74, 70.

12 St Augustine, *Sermon 191*; available here: www.dec25th.info/Augustine%27s%20Sermon%20191.html (accessed 15.8.19).

13 Williams, J., 'O Rex Gentium: O King of the Nations', in *The Church Times* (21 December 2018), available at: www.churchtimes.co.uk/articles/2018/21-december/faith/faith-features/o-rex-gentium-o-king-of-the-nations (accessed 29.3.19).

14 McCabe, *God Matters*, p. 124.

15 McCabe, *God Matters*, p. 124.

16 McCabe, *God Matters*, p. 95.

17 For the limits of the usefulness of the question 'What would Jesus do?' as 'a nice short cut to the truth', see Williams, R., 'The Archbishop of Canterbury's Christmas message to RT readers'; available at www.radiotimes.com/news/2011-12-21/the-archbishop-of-canterburys-christmas-message-to-rt-readers/ (accessed 14.8.19).

18 Bonhoeffer, *Letters*, p. 134.

4

The Wrath of God

> It is not enough for people to be angry – the supreme task is to organize and unite people so that their anger becomes a transforming force. (Martin Luther King)[1]

In this chapter we continue our exploration of the classical attributes of God. We turn now to God's anger.[2] This chapter is designed to make you angry. At the very least, it's designed to rehabilitate the concept of anger theologically. If you finish reading it and are mildly perturbed, it will have gone at least some way to achieving its goal.

This chapter continues our attempt to build a Christian concept of action based on the classical Christian doctrine of God. In what follows, we start by thinking about God's anger, then Christ's, then our own. We do so to prompt reflection about why we should get angry, and how we should utilize that anger to co-operate with God's mission in the world. Ultimately, we suggest the cultivation of a holy anger. Such an anger is a little more like God's anger than the anger that might usually afflict us, and does a little more of what God's anger does, as we shall see below.

The Wrath of God

In much theological discussion, if God's anger is explored at all it tends to be associated with theories of salvation, and some potentially controversial theories of salvation in particular.

Within soteriology – the branch of theology dedicated to exploring how it is we are saved – there is a long-running debate about the extent to which God's anger is 'satisfied' on the cross.

The most obvious example of this debate in contemporary Church life concerns the lyrics to the worship song, 'In Christ Alone'.[3] The line which sparks debate is: 'Till on that cross as Jesus died, the wrath of God was satisfied.' Theologies whose soteriology gives a central place to the wrath of God sing this lyric with little problem. Others reject this lyric for a host of reasons. Defenders of this lyric do not always acknowledge that it is not the concept of God's 'wrath' or the notion of Christ's death 'satisfying' something that troubles those who find this lyric problematic.

The language of wrath is clearly applied to God in the New Testament.[4] Likewise, the language of satisfaction can be rightly applied to the exchange on the cross. On the cross, according to a particular theory of salvation, either the debt which the Devil could reasonably expect to be paid, or our debt to God, is paid. In either of these theories of salvation, Christ's death is a 'ransom' for our salvation.[5]

However, the combination of the concepts of wrath and satisfaction in this lyric are problematic. The combination is not obviously biblical.[6] Moreover, it is not easy to understand how anger, let alone *God's* anger, could be satisfied. If by 'satisfy' the authors of the lyric intend to mean something like 'placate', then we once again face the problem of applying a human understanding of an attribute or emotion to God.

Moreover, it is difficult to see how God *in his anger which needs placating* would wish to give us the means of placating that which needs to be placated. We do not have the space to explore this debate further, except to say that not only does such an understanding of anger divorce it from the other divine attributes, but the notion of anger we uncover below does not easily admit of notions of 'satisfaction'.

Other theological traditions underplay the 'wrath of God' encountered in Scripture and stress instead the nature and extent of God's love. They struggle to think of God being angry at all. There are some commendable reasons for this. We know that God's love is primary. We read in our New Testament not that God is anger, but that he is love.[7] It is out of love for the world that he becomes one of us and redeems us through Christ. Moreover, we know the abuse that has been administered and the fear that has been cultivated in the name of an angry God by irresponsible so-called preachers of the Gospel. Such perversions of the Gospel promote unduly the fear that we are told again and again in Scripture to avoid: 'You did not receive the spirit of slavery to fall back into fear' (Rom. 8.15).[8] We are not saved by fear, but by hope.[9]

However, recognizing this does not mean that we are able to do away with the anger of God attested to in Scripture. What it does mean is that we need to be careful not to fall foul of the ever-present temptation to understand something of God by application of our creaturely experience of the particular emotion or attribute. As St Augustine notes, if we conceive of such qualities, 'as they exist in us, He has none of them'.[10] So too, St Cyril observes that:

> whenever therefore the Divine Scripture wishes to express God's emotion against impious designs of whatever kind, it derives its language as on other occasions from expressions in use among us, and in human phraseology speaks of anger and wrath; although the divine essence is subject to none of these passions in any way that bears comparison with our feelings.[11]

Anger is perhaps the emotion for which we need to be most cautious of applying a human notion to God, given the often toxic nature of uncontrollable bouts of human rage.

The doctrine of divine simplicity we traced above helps us here. The identity of divine attributes suggested by divine simplicity helps us to hold together attributes that appear to be contradictory in their human form. While human anger and human love are distinct, the simplicity of God means that whatever God's anger is, it is identical with his love. God's anger is God's love.[12]

If one grants that God is simple, then God's anger *is* God's love. Here we see our first difference between human and divine anger. Human anger and human love differ because they are different properties or states within the loving woman or angry man. In contrast, divine anger is identical to divine love and differs in how it impacts upon its subject.

This difference of impact, while stemming from the same divine, and simple, source, means that the same divine action in the world can be perceived as love by some and anger by others, depending on their standing in relation to that action. This difference in relation lies behind some understandings of Judgement Day. In such understandings of that fateful day, God isn't petulant or flaky. He doesn't burn some while welcoming others to heaven. God simply acts. He acts so that he is all-in-all; what is outside of Christ doesn't survive the fire of God's love; only what is in Christ will remain, all within the one-and-the-same action of God. To those inside Christ, they experience Love face-to-face. To those outside of Christ, that same action will be perceived as the culmination of divine vengeance. For example, the author of the Pseudo-Clementine *Recognitions* writes: 'that anger, however, which punished the wicked does not bring on disturbance of the mind, but is, I may say, one and the same affection which allots rewards to the good and punishment to the wicked'.[13]

Our problem isn't that God is angry at some people and loves others. Our problem is that we're not very good at working out what God loves and what makes God angry. Rowan Williams reminds us of this with the spiritual he quotes at the end of his *Christian Theology*: 'Nobody knows who I am till judgement morning'.[14] Until we see God face to face, *we* won't be *sure* that we've correctly identified the object and extent of God's love and of his anger. God knows, and that's enough.

St Thomas Aquinas notes that the reason we can speak about divine 'anger' at all is because to us God's anger appears similar to the impact of human anger: 'Anger and the like are attributed to God on account of a similitude of effect.'[15] The disorienting effect we might experience of an angry man appears to us the same as the anger of God in upsetting our comfort and upending our enjoyable status quo. However, human anger and divine anger differ fundamentally in how they impact upon the one who is angry.

Human Anger

We can summarize our exploration of the doctrine of God and divine anger so far: God is simple. God's love is God's anger. Divine anger differs from human anger in that human anger and human love are distinct properties. In God, according to the doctrine of divine simplicity, they are identical.

Another difference between human and divine anger is the extent of their effect. While Aquinas notes that there is a similarity of effect on the object of our anger, human anger primarily affects the *subject* of the anger, the angry woman or man, the person who is angry. Think of an angry person: raised pulse, red face, high blood pressure. Divine anger, meanwhile, transforms the *object* of God's anger.

Deena Grant has shown that in the Hebrew Bible, our Old Testament, the Hebrew word for 'anger' (*chemeh*) when applied to humans describes a state in that person.[16] We see the effect of human anger on its subject rather vividly in Dan. 3.19. Nebuchadnezzar is so filled with 'anger' against Shadrach, Meshach, and Abednego that his face is distorted.

Grant notes that 'whereas human *chemeh* serves as the object of passive verbs that describe the state of being angry (i.e. to be filled with anger), divine *chemeh* serves as the subject of passive verbs that describe the trajectory of anger toward its target'.[17] This is clearest when she looks at the relationship between 'anger' and 'burning'. Human anger burns up the angry person. God's anger burns towards the object of his anger. Our anger changes us, it raises our blood pressure. God's anger changes what he's angry at – God's anger transforms.

Finally, in order to develop the theological basis that we're sketching out, we can look again at the anger of Christ in the New Testament.

Christ's Anger

We know that if we want to see God most clearly in this life, we look to Christ. We know too – how many times have each of us preached – that while it's wrong to be angry, it's okay to be righteously indignant, because Jesus was righteously indignant in the Temple.[18] We see Jesus turning the tables on the money-changers and we teach others that there are some things we can be righteously indignant about. However, most preachers shy away from saying it's ok to be angry, because we assume that Christ could never be *angry*.

We don't let our reading of Scripture interpret our understanding of virtue and our images of Christ. We do let our aversion to anger and the image of Jesus we have in our mind from our childhood – the white-skinned, blue-eyed, blonde-haired holier-than-thou lovely-to-everyone Jesus – interpret our reading of Scripture. This Jesus doesn't get angry, because lovely Jesus *could* never get angry.[19] He gets righteously indignant.

The Jesus we meet on the pages of Scripture ever challenges the Jesus we have in our mind's eye; *Jesus* ever challenges the images and idols we make of him.

When we turn to the New Testament, we find a Jesus somewhat removed from the mild and obedient Jesus of our childhood Christmas carols. The Jesus of Matthew who chides the Scribes and the Pharisees in Matthew 23 does so passionately and, we might say, angrily. He doesn't challenge them inanely, or even particularly *nice*-ly.

The best example of our image of Jesus driving our reading of Scripture, rather than our image of Jesus being challenged by it, is in the raising of Lazarus in John 11. This is a vital passage of Scripture for our theologies of healing and in speaking to our society's aversion to the penultimate reality of death.

The episode doesn't start well. You can sense Jesus' frustration with the disciples. 'Our friend Lazarus has fallen asleep, but I am going there to awaken him' (John 11.11). 'The disciples said to him, "Lord, if he has fallen asleep, he will be all right." ... Then Jesus told them plainly, "Lazarus is dead"' (John 11.12, 14).

Then Jesus arrives at Bethany and Mary and Martha are grieving. He sees Mary crying tears of grief and the Jews with her weeping. And he was *greatly disturbed in spirit and deeply moved* (John 11.33). He weeps (John 11.35). He arrives at the tomb and is again *greatly disturbed* (11.38). Jesus is sad at the death of his friend. Lovely Jesus.

Except that when we look at the Greek, our image of Jesus is challenged. *Embrimaomai* (ἐμβριμάομαι), translated here in the New Revised Standard Version as 'greatly disturbed in spirit' and 'deeply moved', is more usually rendered 'snorting with anger' and 'deeply agitated'. We let our image of Jesus drive our translation. We can't bring ourselves to say 'Jesus is angry'. We water this down: Jesus is 'greatly disturbed in spirit'. We don't let *our* view of what it means to be good be challenged by the Jesus that actually meets us in Scripture. And what happens when Jesus gets angry? Stuff happens. Jesus' anger transforms the situation. Lazarus is raised and through this many believe – in Jesus, and that death, though inevitable, is not the end.

All this shouldn't surprise us. We believe Jesus is the Incarnate God. If we believe in a God whose anger is identical to his love, then we shouldn't be surprised when we see Jesus exhibiting a kind of anger *and* when that anger looks a lot like divine anger – anger that transforms not the person who is angry but the object of his anger. Jesus' anger transforms the death of Lazarus, bringing him back to life and many to believe.

There's one more thing worth noting in this passage. Jesus weeps. If Jesus' tears are like the Jews' tears, they're both sad at the death of their friend. But the whole point of this passage is that the Jews' tears are a sign that they don't understand what the life of Jesus means for the death of us all. Jesus' tears occur between two references to his anger. Jesus' tears aren't divorced from his anger, they are bound up with it. Jesus is crying as much at the disbelief of his friends as at the death of one of them. Jesus cries with and because of that which makes him angry. His grief is tied up with his anger.

Anger and Grief

Grief and anger are intimately bound. Our word 'anger' comes from the Old Norse word for grief.[20] John Shore notes that:

> The root of our word anger is, in fact, the Old Norse word *angr*, which means anguish, distress, grief, sorrow, affliction. And I wasn't surprised to discover that's so, because in its purest, most concentrated form – which is to say when it's attended by perfect helplessness – that's what anger is: anguish.[21]

If nothing else, our anger is our sadness that the world in which we live is not the world as it might be, that the world in which we live is not the world that God ultimately intends it to be. We can and should get angry at those things that grieve us in the world, that make us sad that they are not as they might be.

Shore also points to something else important here, about the relation between anger and helplessness. What makes us angry isn't only what makes us grieve. What makes us angry is also those situations that we feel powerless to do anything about.

Human anger, when appropriately directed, has the potential to be transformed into a divine anger, and this sort of anger, as we have seen, has the potential to transform.

Transforming Anger

In short, we shouldn't just stop at getting angry. Just as God's anger transforms that with which he is angry, as God's anger transforms us, as God's love transforms us, so our anger can be transformative.

Methodist lay preacher and founding politician of the Labour movement, Keir Hardie, once described his life as 'stirring up divine discontent with wrong'. We shouldn't just allow whims of anger to be transformational. We should be intentional about cultivating a holy anger, in ourselves and in our churches. We should whip up divine discontent with the wrongs we discern in all the ways that the world and our society fail to promote the flourishing of each and every person in accordance with God's will.

How do we go about this? How can we make our helplessness, our grief, our anger at this like God's anger? How can we cultivate a holy anger, a divine discontent that might begin to speak into our communities and transform them?

Martin Luther King helps us again here:

Now, we got to get this thing right. What is needed is a realization that power without love is reckless and abusive, and that love without power is sentimental and anaemic. Power at its best is love implementing the demands of justice, and justice at its best is love correcting everything that stands against love.[22]

King reminds us elsewhere that for our anger to be transformative it needs to have impact: 'It is not enough for people to be angry – the supreme task is to organize and unite people so that their anger becomes a transforming force.'[23] If our anger is to have impact we need power. Without such power all our efforts, notes King, risk being sentimental or anaemic.

Power

Talk of power often makes Christians itchy, and 'power' can all too quickly be dismissed as an un-Christian notion. This is lazy thinking that plays into the hands of those who have power in our world.

In the same essay from which we quoted above, Williams notes 'we are not talking about a repudiation of the whole notion of power, as a hasty reading of the tradition might suggest, but about how the creative and transfiguring power of God is actually seen in our world'.[24]

Just as our anger should be like God's anger, our power should be like God's power. And just as God's anger is transformative, so obviously is his power. Christians shouldn't be afraid of power, but they *should* be afraid of holding power in a human way and not in God's. Power is simply the ability to act – to do, or to get others to do or stop doing something. King has already told us what power looks like when it's exercised like God's, when our use of power might become a transforming force. We have power when we organize and unite people.

Human power organizes, controls and divides. God's power unites. Christians utilize this power when they organize and unite people around God's vision for community, and not a vision of our own devising.

If we organize and unite people around our holy anger, around God's vision for community, and around that sense of anger or grief or frustration where the world falls short of this vision, where it is not what it might be, then we begin to build our capacity to act, to live out that vision. We build our power.

We build communities and institutions and churches motivated by a common discontent that the world is not as it could be. A common anger that there are more who have yet to hear the good news of Jesus, that there are those in our parishes not living that life in all its fullness that God intends, that there are entire families and communities that are not free to live the lives that God wills them to live. A common anguish that there are those in our parishes held in bondage by the chains of poverty, or by the greed, selfishness, and idolatry of others, those with the ability to act in such a way that those chains might no longer hold them back. A common grief that there are those in our midst who might even today begin to share in the abundance of the Risen Life.

If we cultivate this holy anger it has the potential to be a transforming force in our community and a means to realize the power we already have to make those voices heard. Like God's anger this holy anger has the power to begin to transform our world and our community around us. As climate change ever reminds us, it is a lie that our actions are not transformative.[25] All of our actions impact the world and those around us. Just as we saw in considering God's intentional suffering in order to redeem suffering, the cultivation of this holy anger requires us to be intentional about the impact of our actions, and to seek to act to transform the situation that gives rise to our holy anger.

A final word on power. God's power, the power we're called to have, relinquishes and transforms, as we saw above in considering God's love. Human power takes for itself and maintains. God's power builds up and is eternal. Human power holds up, corrupts and moreover all around us is, literally, decaying; this is why it's so vital that we act as a community of faith.

As Moises Naím notes in his *The End of Power*:

Power is undergoing a far more fundamental mutation that has not been sufficiently recognized and understood. Even as rival states, companies, political parties, social movements, and institutions or individual leaders fight for power as they have done throughout the ages, power itself – what they are fighting so desperately to get and keep – is slipping away. *Power is decaying* ... It is a picture of power scattered among an increasing number of newer, smaller players from diverse and unexpected origins.[26]

Power implies the ability to act. The shifts in power that Naím has identified have both undermined the ability of the Church to utilize the power it once held (however justly or unjustly it used that power) and also prevented the Church from fulfilling one aspect of its vocation. The decay of power has limited both the Church's ability to be a buffer against the forces and worldly powers that affect the lives of its members, and also its ability to be a training ground for how individuals should hold power and act in a way that God intends.[27] These shifts in power have undermined the ability of churches and other intermediary institutions to train their members in how to organize and bring people together to transform their communities with a common vision of what the world might be.

The community organizer Ernesto Cortes notes:

> Long before recent terrorist attacks, invasions, economic downturns, and hurricanes, the alienating and homogenizing effects of globalization and the dominant market culture had begun to isolate people from one another and from their institutions, destroying our relationality and creating a new kind of tribalism ... The intermediary institutions in which we are taught the habits and practices requisite for a vibrant democratic culture. These institutions would have enabled us to develop the social knowledge to act effectively to counter the demagoguery of both parties in the public arena. Without these institutions, we are reduced to self-absorbed narcissism, which easily appropriates the language of consumerism and individualism.[28]

He goes on:

> As a result, the real conversations of engagement – of listening, and particularly of listening to the other person as another, as someone with a different perspective, a different point of view, a different story or history – rarely take place anymore. Yet it is only through these kinds of conversations

that people develop the capacity to think long-term, to consider something outside of their own experience, to reconsider their own experience, and to develop a larger vision of their neighbourhood, their state, or their society. Unfortunately people don't develop the capacity to have deliberative conversations on their own.[29]

These shifts in power have broken down relationships and isolated individuals within our community – as the increasing problems of isolation and loneliness demonstrate only too well. In doing so, they have made the lives of those in our churches more vulnerable to the visions of community – if they even have a real vision of community – of developers and corporations they will never see, to visions of community in which they have no real say or creative role. The buffer intermediary institutions such as those the Church provided have been undermined, and places for learning the skills and habits of community, for building and delivering on a vision of what the world might be, have vanished in this new world order.

This *should* make us angry. What are we to do?

We need to strengthen this buffer. Matthew Bolton in his *How To Resist* notes:

> In times past, the churches played perhaps the most significant role. If we think of some of the great institutions we benefit from today – hospitals, schools, housing associations, trade unions and charities – these were often developed in, or sponsored by, local churches. As the primary gathering place of a local community, connecting with each other around a tradition of hope and service, the churches gave birth to many of the great social innovations and also many of the great social justice campaigns, such as the abolition of slavery ... We still desperately need faith communities to play this role.[30]

If as Christians we allow our anger to be like God's, we begin to build transformative communities that share our dissatisfaction that the world is not as it might be, and not as God wills it. Cortes notes that justice 'emerges when all parties with a stake in the question are involved in the deliberation'.[31] Even sharing and giving voice to common frustrations and concerns is making the world a little more as God wishes it to be. As members of local churches we are in a position to hear the voices and contributions of those who are often overlooked by public consultations and listening exercises. Even as we share with each other more of these stories of the way the world really is, we are building our power as we build connections and relationships between individuals and communities that strengthen our ability to act, and serve as a buffer to the decay and abuses of power around us.

And how do we do this?

By cultivating holy anger – by allowing ourselves to be frustrated where the world is not what it might be and not how God wishes it to be.

The poet Carolyn Forché, in her immensely moving *What You Have Heard is True*, an account of the build-up to the civil war in El Salvador and the assassination of St Oscar Romero, recounts advice given to her: 'You have to be able to see the world as it is, to see how it is put together, and you have to be able to say what you see. And get angry.'[32] The argument of this chapter has been that our anger needs to be like God's. We need to cultivate an anger that doesn't lead to us getting red-faced and doing nothing. We need to cultivate an anger that sees the way the world really is and gets angry at it, and utilizes that anger as a transforming force. This involves seeing the world as it really is, communicating that vision, and sharing and spreading that holy anger. This requires 'stirring up divine discontent with wrong', to use Keir Hardie's phrase.

Such godly anger, like the godly love we explored in the previous chapter, requires the whole of ourselves. Forché recounts witnessing St Oscar Romero celebrating the Sunday Mass in

the presence of the coffins at the altar of those murdered that
week, and listing the names of those who had disappeared:

> [Romero] walked toward the coffins with an aspergillum,
> sprinkling holy water on the dead, and then he walked through
> the congregation ... the water sprinkling down on our bowed
> heads as it had on the coffins. Later I would understand that
> here the dead and the living were together, and those who
> stood alive before him he was blessing in advance.[33]

Few of us reading these words are called to live out our
Christian calling in contexts that will mean almost certain
suffering and death. Many of our brothers and sisters in Christ
live the daily reality of the risk of being killed at any moment
on account of their faith. Many, if not most, of our fellow
human beings live in contexts where their lives are at daily risk.
All of us are required to give the whole of ourselves in love
in the face of a world that seeks to destroy love wherever it
breaks in. All of us are called to transform our world according
to that pattern of love laid down for us in Christ, to conform
more closely to God's will, to end the cycles of destruction and
death in which we remain trapped.

I want to end this chapter on a note of hope. As Christians,
we are in our local communities and contexts for the long
game. Power is decaying. The world as we know it is passing
away. Even those sources of oppression and misinformation
which seem impossible to overcome are passing away, and will
likely pass away sooner than the rest of the world around us.

As churches with a vision of our community, a shared vision
of what the world might be, we can position ourselves to challenge and step into those spaces where earthly power decays,
which might otherwise be left to rack and ruin. Even if we feel
powerless in the face of all this now, we know that nothing
in this world lasts forever. Only the Creator is eternal. In the
meantime, we've got quite enough to be angry about.

Notes

1 King, M. L., *"Honoring Mr Dubois" Carnegie Hall Tribute to Dr. W.E.B. Dubois on the 100th Anniversary of His Birth in February* (1968); available at www.ushistory.org/documents/dubois.htm (accessed 15.8.19).

2 An earlier version of this chapter was published as Cuff, S., 'Turning the Tables: Transforming Anger to Action', in *Crucible* (January 2019), pp. 41–51.

3 Townend, S. and Getty, K., 'In Christ Alone' (2001), © Capitol Christian Music Group.

4 Matt. 3.7; John 3.36; Rom. 1.18 + *passim*; Eph. 5.6; 1 Thess. 1.10; Rev. 11.18; cf. Rev. 6.16.

5 Cf. Mark 10.45; Matt. 20.28; 1 Tim. 2.6.

6 See Paul, I., 'On the cross when Jesus died, was "the wrath of God satisfied"?' (12 August 2013); available at www.psephizo.com/biblical-studies/on-the-cross-when-jesus-died-was-the-wrath-of-god-satisfied/ (accessed 20.8.19).

7 1 John 4.8, 16.

8 Matt. 10.31; Luke 12.7, 32; 1 John 4.18; cf. Luke 1.74; 12.5; 2 Cor. 7.5; Phil. 1.14.

9 Rom. 8.24.

10 Augustine, *On Patience* 1.1; available at: www.newadvent.org/fathers/1315.htm (accessed 17.8.19).

11 Cyril, *Commentary on John* 12.6, cited in Gavrilyuk, 'God's Impassible Suffering in the Flesh', p. 60.

12 Moltmann makes a similar observation: 'Love is the source and the basis of the possibility of the wrath of God. The opposite of love is not wrath, but indifference. Indifference towards justice and injustice would be a retreat on the part of God from the covenant. But his wrath is an expression of his abiding interest in man' (*The Crucified God*, p. 272). On the relationship between love and indifference see Nebel, M., 'Transforming Unjust Structures: A Philosophical and Theological Perspective', in *Political Theology* 12.1 (2011), pp. 118–43.

13 Pseudo-Clement, *Recognitions* 10.48, cited in Gavrilyuk, *Impassible*, p. 54. This text purports to be written by the first-century Clement; however, it is generally dated to the fourth century CE.

14 Williams, R., 'Nobody Knows Who I Am 'Till Judgement Morning', in *On Christian Theology* (Oxford: Blackwell, 2000), pp. 276–89.

15 Aquinas, *Summa* I.3.2; available at www.newadvent.org/summa/1003.htm (accessed 13.8.19).

16 Grant, D., 'Brief Discussion of the Difference between Human and Divine חמה', in *Biblica* 91.3 (2010), 418–24.

17 Grant, 'Brief Discussion', p. 421.

18 Mark 11.15–19; Matt. 21.12–17; Luke 19.4–48; John 2.14–21.

19 See Lester, A. D., *The Angry Christian: A Theology for Care and Counselling* (Louisville, KY: Westminster John Knox Press, 2013), especially pp. 150–66 for a sustained attempt to rehabilitate the concept of anger. I'm indebted to Sue Colman for pointing me towards Lester's work.

20 I'm indebted to Charlotte Fischer for pointing out this etymology.

21 Shore, J., 'Christian woman: "She's pulled the plug on her own son, whom I love and cared for. How do I deal with my anger?"' (29 March 2012); available at: https://www.patheos.com/blogs/john shore/2012/03/shes-pulled-the-plug-her-own-son-whom-i-love-help/ (accessed 20.8.19).

22 King, M. L., *"Where Do We Go From Here?" Annual Report Delivered at the 11th Convention of the Southern Christian Leadership Conference, Atlanta, GA* (16 August 1967); available at: www.stanford.edu/group/King/publications/speeches/Where_do_we_go_from_here.html (accessed 15.8.19).

23 King, 'Mr Dubois'.

24 Williams, 'Nobody Knows', p. 288.

25 On climate change, see especially Pope Francis, *Laudato Si', On Care For Our Common Home*; available at: w2.vatican.va/content/francesco/en/encyclicals/documents/papa-francesco_20150524_enciclica-laudato-si.html (accessed 15.8.19).

26 Naím, M., *The End of Power: From Boardrooms to Battlefields* (New York: Basic Books, 2013), pp. 1–2.

27 On the role of churches and other intermediary institutions for training people to engage more widely in society and the transformation of society see Cuff, S., 'Subsidiarity', in *Love in Action: Catholic Social Teaching for Every Church* (London: SCM Press, 2019), pp. 88–107.

28 Cortes, E., 'Toward a Democratic Culture', in *Kettering Review* (Spring 2006), pp. 46–57, 46.

29 Cortes, 'Democratic Culture', p. 46.

30 Bolton, M., *How To Resist* (London: Bloomsbury, 2018), pp. 10–11.

31 Cortes, 'Democratic Culture', p. 48.

32 Forché, C., *What You Have Heard is True: A Memoir of Witness and Resistance* (New York: Penguin, 2019), p. 274.

33 Forché, *What You Have Heard*, p. 194.

5

The Mercy of God

Attend to mercy and justice. Do not imagine that these two can be separated in any way. They may at first seem to be mutually opposed, so that whoever is merciful would not uphold justice and whoever adheres unconditionally to justice would forget about mercy. But God is omnipotent: he lets go of neither justice in showing mercy nor mercy in judging justly. (St Augustine)[1]

In the last chapter we considered the anger of God. We saw how God's love *is* God's anger, and how that anger is a force that transforms that with which God is angry. We suggested that our anger should likewise be transformative and contribute to building the kind of world that God is ever calling into being.

We now turn to consider the justice and mercy of God. These concepts are often thought of in relation to God's anger. When God's anger is viewed as a projection of human anger, God has a right to be so angry because of his justice. He won't be angry easily or for very long because of his mercy. He is 'slow to anger and abounding in steadfast love' as we read throughout our Old Testament.[2] While he won't get angry easily, there are justified limits that if crossed will incur God's wrath.

Our exploration of God's anger suggested that projecting human anger onto God won't do. Unlike us, God isn't a passive subject to his anger. Rather, God's anger transforms the situations with which he is angry. He is not slow to transformation. Likewise, God is not merely a patient but distant observer of our actions, who overlooks as much as he can before exacting judgement.

The idea that God is slow to anger and quick to mercy is well expressed in the sentiment of a famous hymn by the Roman Catholic Fr Frederick Faber (1814–63): 'There's a wideness in God's mercy'.[3] This hymn is often sung in such a way that it makes God sound like an avuncular sort of chap that you'd be keen to have a pint with, a thoroughly nice bloke who's kind to everyone, wouldn't hurt a fly. This image of the kindly God is a positive one compared to the more harmful images of an angry God which we discussed in the previous chapter.

The images we have of God in our mind's eye are often those we've picked up from childhood or the world around us. They can be seemingly inane, like the image of God as a nice bloke, or they can be harmful, like the image of a god who engenders only fear. Such images can turn us away altogether from living in relationship with God. Even the seemingly inane 'nice guy' image of God can have harmful consequences. This sort of god in our mind's eye anthropomorphizes the divine, makes a god in our own image and, more perniciously, furthers the lie of the superiority of maleness.

All of our images fall short of the reality of the living God. In this book we have already encountered the theological tradition of negative theology, or in technical terms 'apophatic'. Such theology is rightly very suspicious of giving space to any of the images or conceptions of God we can form for ourselves.

When we come to think about God's justice and mercy these images are at the forefront of our mind. The angry god and the lovely god battle against each other in our mind's eye, and depending on our temperament, we're as likely to pick one over the other. This means that either we end up with a god who is an exacting judge or a god who turns a blind eye to our misdeeds.

Scripture and the tradition of Christian orthodoxy hold God's justice and mercy together in the kind of creative tension that, as we have seen, is often a feature of the grammar of orthodox Christian thought. Passages emphasizing God's mercy sit alongside passages emphasizing God's exacting justice. So, for example, Jeremiah 3.2 ('I will not look on you in anger, for I am merciful, says the Lord; I will not be angry for ever') sits alongside Psalm 37.28 ('the Lord loves justice; he will not forsake his saints. The righteous shall be preserved for ever, but the children of the wicked shall be cut off').

Likewise, passages implying a divisive judgement of humankind sit alongside passages that strongly suggest that God wants all people to be saved. So, for example, Matthew 25.46 ('these will go away into eternal punishment, but the righteous into eternal life') sits alongside 1 Timothy 2.3-4: ('God our Saviour who desires everyone to be saved').

This presents us with a conundrum. Scripture seems to assert both a decisive judgement and the salvation of all, sometimes referred to as '*apokatastasis panton*' or the restoration of all.

Justice and Mercy

If it is true, as the first letter to Timothy tells us, that God desires all people to be saved, we usually think that God gets what God wills. This is what we mean when we talk of God's omnipotence or his ability to do anything. We read elsewhere in Scripture that 'for God all things are possible' (Matt. 19.26). If God desires all people to be saved, the salvation of all people is at least within the realms of possibility, given God's omnipotence. Whereas the Rolling Stones were right as far as humankind goes when they sang, 'you can't always get what you want', Christian orthodoxy generally suggests that God can.

Recalling the doctrine of divine simplicity, we remember that whatever God's justice is, it is identical to his mercy. God is God, and God is just, and God is merciful. God's justice is God's mercy. God's judgement is God's mercy. As Josef Pieper notes: 'these qualities in God, which to the creature appear to be contradictory, are actually identical'.[4] It's not that God is kind to some and exacting with others, but that whatever God's judgement means and whatever God's mercy means they are from the one and the same pure act of God being God. We can recall the words of Pseudo-Clement from the previous chapter: 'one and the same affection which allots rewards to the good and punishment to the wicked'.[5]

We have already alluded to the question of universal salvation in discussing the problem of reconciling God's omnipotence – his desire for all to be saved – with those passages of Scripture which seem to suggest a decisive judgement. Even raising the subject of universal salvation – the potential for all to be saved – results in strong reactions on the part of some Christians.[6] It invites the accusation of departing from Scripture, even though we have already seen that there are scriptural grounds for investigating the possibility. Moreover, there are further scriptural grounds for suggesting the *possibility* of the salvation of all. These are primarily Christological, based on the universality of what God has done for us in Christ: 'as in Adam all die, so also in Christ shall all be made alive' (1 Cor. 15.22). Even passages that have long been utilized in the service of the notion of a predestined elect few can be utilized in support of the salvation of all because of the universality of God's foreknowledge of all those he creates: 'for those whom he foreknew he also predestined to be conformed to the image of his Son, in order that he might be the firstborn within a large family' (Rom. 8.29). When taken alongside passages such as Isaiah 49.1 or Psalm 139.13, which indicate the intimacy of God's knowledge of us from before we were born, who is it that God has not foreknown and therefore predestined?

There are, however, strong grounds for resisting the proclamation of universal salvation, as we shall see. Nevertheless, we should be cautious of strong reactions *against* universal salvation. The human instinct for both tribalism and being treated fairly is so strong that the twin suggestion implied by universal salvation – that it does not matter which tribe you are in, and that those outside or new to your tribe will be treated in the same way as you – engenders a strong reaction. Within the New Testament, the parable of the workers in the vineyard in Matthew's Gospel (20.1–16) seems to be directed precisely against the affront to our human sense of fairness that late-comers will get the same reward as those who have believed the Gospel from the outset. Given the strength of our human instincts, we should be wary if our opposition to the salvation of all stems from the instinct to tribalism, the affront to our sense of fairness, or the human desire for power and control which means that we want to view our faith not as gift but as the result of *our* correct decision.

Indeed, it should strike us as odd that we as Christians are so ready to condemn the possibility of everyone being saved. If it is God's will that all are saved, the energy which is generated by those who object to the possibility of universal salvation in opposing those Christians who preach it could be better spent in hoping and praying for the salvation of all that God desires. Indeed, we shall see that hope and prayer for the salvation of all is the most we can responsibly affirm, given the witness of Scripture.

First, however, we must consider the case against affirming the salvation of all. There are two main grounds that prevent us from affirming that God's justice and mercy result in the salvation of all. The first has to do with our exercise of judgement and the second with God's freedom to judge, but both are related.

We read in Scripture that we are not to judge: 'Do not judge, so that you may not be judged. For with the judgement you make you will be judged, and the measure you give will be the measure you get' (Matt. 7.1–2). So too in Luke's Gospel we are told to 'Be merciful, just as your Father is merciful. Do not judge, and you will not be judged; do not condemn, and you will not be condemned' (Luke 6.36–7). It is beyond our human limitations to judge with the righteous judgement of God who alone can see the heart and test the mind. This prevents us from one aspect of the mechanism of human tribalism that we so enjoy: declaring insiders and outsiders, who's in and who's out. Christ in his flesh tears down such barriers.[7] As Rowan Williams notes, 'the history of Jesus enacts a judgement on tribalism and self-protecting religion'.[8] We are unable to judge who is saved and who is not because God in Christ alone is judge.[9]

So while our inability to judge prevents us from declaring judgement on who's in and who's out, it also prevents us from declaring that all are in. To declare that none are saved or some are saved or all are saved is to put ourselves in God's place and to usurp the role of God as judge.

The second objection to proclaiming the salvation of all is related to the first. This objection is based on God's freedom. God must be free to save all or save some or save none at all. When considering whether God might be so merciful as to deliver on his will for all to be saved by bringing all to salvation, Karl Barth (1886–1968) famously stops short of proclaiming this as the case. He states that we can neither say God will save all of us nor can we say that he will not save all of us. Instead, in a passage worth quoting in full, Barth proclaims the freedom of God to decide either way:

> *God's free grace*. Because it is free, it has the power to do its work even among us miserable sinners ... David the adulterer and murderer was no hindrance to it, nor was Peter the denier, nor Saul the persecutor ... We may trust [God's free grace] to be more powerful than us as Christians, than the ocean of nonsense which precisely we Christians commit individually and collectively. Why should we not rely upon it? It is and will prove itself once again to be much more powerful than everything which the children of this world, in their absurdity and disobedience, can set against it ... Who knows what sort of 'last' ones might turn out to be first again? The proclamation of the Church must allow for this freedom of grace. *Apokatastasis panton?* No, for a grace which automatically

would ultimately have to embrace each and every one would certainly not be free grace. It surely would not be God's grace. But would it be God's free grace if we could absolutely deny that it could do that? Has Christ been sacrificed only for our sins? Has He not, according to 1 John 2:2, been sacrificed for the whole world? Strange Christianity, whose most pressing anxiety seems to be that God's grace might prove to be all too free on this side, that hell, instead of being populated with so many people, might some day prove to be empty![10]

Hans Urs von Balthasar (1905–1988), the Roman Catholic theologian, arrives at a similar position from a close reading of the scriptural witness, while ultimately rejecting Barth's own account as too close to a proclamation of salvation for all.[11] In his *Dare We Hope That All Men Be Saved*, von Balthasar surveys the New Testament witness and finds a general trend toward a decisive judgement pre-Easter and a trend towards the salvation of all in reflection on the Christ-event post Easter, that ultimately cannot be reconciled into a clear affirmation either way:

Predominantly pre-Easter aspects cannot be merged with the post-Easter ones into a readily comprehensible system; that the fear of the possibility of being lost, as called for by the first series of texts, is by no means superseded, in favour of a knowledge of the outcome of judgement, by those of the second aspect; but that the Old Testament image of judgement – which, with few exceptions, is strictly two-sided – may well have become clearer (the Judge is the Saviour of all) and that, as a result, hope outweighs fear ... [It] should not, therefore – as in system-building theses such as those put forward by Karl Barth – be interpreted as meaning that Jesus, as God's chosen One, is rejected in the place of all sinners, 'so that, besides him, no one may be lost' (Barth, *Church Dogmatics*, II/1). This comment is, to be sure, surrounded by others whose tone is less absolute, and the term apokatastasis, or 'universal reconciliation', is carefully avoided, even rejected. Still one ought to stay well away from so systematic a statement and limit oneself to that Christian hope that does not mask a concealed knowing but rests essentially content with the Church's prayer, as called for in 1 Tim. 2:4, that God wills that all men be saved.[12]

However, von Balthasar overplays the distinction between his own position and Barth's. Barth's position is essentially negative: we can't proclaim universal salvation nor can we not proclaim it. Balthasar's position is grounded in a more prayerful optimism: 'that Christian hope that does not mark a concealed knowing'. Balthasar ends up on genuine hope, and the prayer that all will be saved.

Von Balthasar's vision of hope is not fanciful hope or mere wishful thinking. Instead, his notion of hope is a means of understanding the relationship between God's justice and his mercy. His last chapter in *Dare We Hope That All Men Be Saved* explores the relationship between these two seemingly contradictory aspects of God's character. It amounts to a brief survey of patristic and medieval thought on the relationship between justice and mercy. In this chapter he points to St Anselm's (1033–1109) treatment of justice and mercy in his *Proslogion*.[13]

St Anselm's discussion of mercy is valuable for the argument of this book. He considers how God can be both merciful and impassible. His solution, like that of Aquinas with respect to anger, is to find that what we call God's 'mercy' is derived from its impact on us and how to us it appears similar in its effect to human mercy.[14] His answer to the mystery of why it is not an affront to God's justice that God in his mercy spares any number of the wicked is based on his fundamental understanding of God's justice.[15] If God spares the wicked he does so, contrary to our understanding of justice as fairness or 'just deserts', precisely *because* he is just. Anselm bases this on the justness of God's will; whatever God wills must be just because God only wills justice.[16] Mercy and justice are not in opposition in God.

Von Balthasar then turns to Aquinas's discussion of justice and mercy in his *Summa Theologica*.[17] Von Balthasar points out that Aquinas's own understanding of justice and mercy in God is inspired by the argument found in Anselm's *Proslogion*.[18] Whereas Anselm bases the identity of God's justice and mercy on the just will of God, Aquinas bases their identity on the priority of mercy, so that God's justice becomes a feature of God's mercy.[19] This idea requires a little unpacking, and is based in part on Aquinas's wider understanding of justice.

For Aquinas, justice is a kind of relationship. Herbert McCabe puts this simply: 'Justice, for Aquinas is the stable disposition to give everyone his or her due; it is concerned with maintaining an equality between people ... Justice, then, is essentially about a relation to another and its criteria are objective.'[20]

Justice is what we owe each other. As a human being I can expect to be in right relationship with those people and things around me. If I'm torn out of that relationship through the sinful acts of others, it's my right to expect to be allowed back into right relationship, or to be put back into right relationship if it's outside my capability.

God's justice is similar, notes Aquinas, in that it means that God gives us what we are owed or what is our due. Aquinas cites Pseudo-Dionysius (whom we encountered in our discussion of divine simplicity above): 'We must needs see that God is truly just, in seeing how He gives to all existing things what is proper to the condition of each.'[21] However, Aquinas argues that God's justice presupposes God's mercy, because you cannot continue the chain of who owes what to whom to infinity; at some point you reach God's mercy and goodness in creating anything at all.

Justice – giving each one their due – presupposes that there is one to whom their due may be given. Creation is an act of God's mercy and goodness. Therefore, God's justice flows from God's mercy, because God's mercy is at work in every act of God's justice by virtue of his creation of that towards which he appears just.[22] In fact, because God's goodness is primary, Aquinas goes further, arguing that God exceeds merely what is owed to his creatures in his relation to them:

> God out of abundance of His goodness bestow[s] upon creatures what is due to them more bountifully than is proportionate to their deserts: since less would suffice for preserving the order of justice than what the divine goodness confers; because between creatures and God's goodness there can be no proportion.[23]

Both Anselm and Aquinas base their belief in the identity of God's justice and his mercy on the nature of God himself, and on his fundamental goodness. Both recognize there is a gulf between our instinctive notions of justice and mercy and those that exist identically in God. Aquinas ends his discussion by emphasizing the superabundance of God's goodness towards us. Von Balthasar, meanwhile, ends his discussion by making hope the solid ground through which we may be able to view the relationship between God's justice and mercy in a clearer light. He does so through a citation of Josef Pieper:

> One who looks only at the justice of God is as little able to hope as is one who sees only the mercy of God. Both fall prey to hopelessness – one to the hopelessness of despair, the other to the hopelessness of presumption. Only hope is able to comprehend the reality of God that surpasses all antitheses, to know that his mercy is identical with his justice and his justice with his mercy.[24]

In our introduction we noted how each of us is liable to distort our understanding of God by focusing on one or other of the aspects of God's character or his attributes. Pieper reminds us of the importance of hope in breaking us out of the distortion of such antitheses, that hope which is grounded in the reality of God himself who surpasses all such antitheses.

Here we can conclude our exploration of God's justice and mercy with the realization that we will never be in a position to discern who is in and who is out of the reaches of God's justice and mercy. Indeed, as Williams noted, God invites us to break out of the human instinct to divide ourselves according to such tribal lines. Instead, we are called on to hope and pray that all may one day be recipients of God's saving mercy. Any account of Christian action must include that for which we are called to pray, and it seems that there is no good reason that such an account should not also include the prayer that each and every one might one day be saved. However, to assert that it is definitely the case that all are saved or to deny that it is even possible both rob our Christian confession of the ground of hope. We cannot hope for what is definitely or impossibly the case.

It is 'in hope we were saved. Now hope that is seen is not hope. For who hopes for what is seen? But if we hope for what we do not see, we wait for it with patience' (Rom. 8.24–5). Pope Benedict XVI (born 1927), in his *Spe Salvi*, reflects on the nature of this hope: 'what sort of hope could ever justify the statement that, on the basis of that hope and simply because it exists, we are redeemed? And what sort of certainty is involved here?'[25] He finds that Christian hope acquires a new kind of certainty because of God's revelation of himself to us in Christ: 'in Christ, God has revealed himself. He has already communicated to us the "substance" of things to come, and thus the expectation of God acquires a new certainty.'[26] As we saw in our explorations of God's love for us, God's gift of himself for us in Christ reveals to us the basis of the Christian life.

In this light we can now look again at the words of Faber's famous hymn, and see that it in fact presents us with an image of God that is far from the kindly avuncular deity that we suggested above this hymn brought to mind. When we look more closely, we see that Faber's hymn is as much about mercy and justice as it is about the liberty of God: 'There's a wideness in God's mercy, like the wideness of the sea; there's a kindness in his justice, which is more than liberty.'[27]

God's mercy is wide, and his justice more than simply God's freedom to do as he pleases. In this respect, Faber goes further than Barth, who maintains God must be so free. Faber reminds us that God's justice transcends even our notions of God's freedom to act justly as God wishes. God's liberty isn't the kind of liberty that makes God reckless, free to do as he pleases, but it is that liberty which in theological terms we know as Grace. In Williams' terms the liberty of Christian Grace means 'the liberty to act, to heal and to create community "outside the gates" of religious practice that has become oppressive or exclusive – God's liberty'.[28] Grace, the liberty of God, is the free gift he offers us in the Christian life. Grace is that free gift which is given to all humankind in Christ.

Faber's hymn is really a meditation on the extent of this Grace: 'grace enough for thousands of new worlds as great as this; there is room for fresh creations in that upper home of bliss'.[29] In reflecting on God's Grace, Faber takes us back to the upper room in which humankind was given the pledge of the gift of the Sacrament of Christ's Body and Blood, the institution of the Eucharist, the gift of Christ himself. Faber's hymn reminds us that all theology begins and ends with Christ.

Faber's hymn was originally published as 'Come to Jesus' and includes the words 'Pining souls come nearer Jesus, and oh come not doubting thus, but with faith that trusts more bravely his huge tenderness for us.'[30] God's mercy is God's justice. God has revealed himself to us uniquely in Christ. Christ is God's mercy and God's judgement. Here too we encounter freedom. Not just that freedom of God to which Barth pointed us, but our freedom in Christ. 'It was for freedom that Christ set us free' (Gal. 5.1). God's free gift gives us our freedom.

In Christ, God shows us his mercy and enacts his judgement. In Christ, we find our freedom – the true freedom for which we were created. In Christ we are freed from our instinctive human tribalism and the relentless logic of who's in and who's out. In Christ, the image of God is restored in us and we are free to live out our share of the risen life.

This is the Christian life. Not fearing God's judgement, or presuming his mercy, but rejoicing in hope at our share in the free gift of Christ himself. Faber was confident that if we lived that life today, all would be well: 'If our love were but more simple, we should take Him at His word; and our lives would be all sunshine in the sweetness of our Lord.'[31]

Fr Faber was more than a little optimistic here. As we saw above in our exploration of suffering, we know that human life in general and the Christian life in particular isn't all sunshine. In Christ we'll have our fair share of knocks and scrapes, and we may well be called upon to give of ourselves in situations where it is difficult to see any sunshine at all. We don't experience an end of suffering in this life. God's free gift to us doesn't free us from death, but through it. We get to Easter Sunday through Good Friday. In the midst of the darknesses and trials of this life, we know that God in Christ is with us sharing *our* suffering. He is God with us as he transforms *our* suffering from the inside.

But Fr Faber was right. Not only is God simple, but so too is the whole of the Christian life. If our love were as simple as the God we worship, we'd take him at his word:

> Come to me, all you that are weary and are carrying heavy burdens, and I will give you rest. Take my yoke upon you, and learn from me; for I am gentle and humble in heart, and you will find rest for your souls. For my yoke is easy, and my burden is light. (Matthew 11.28–30)

Reflecting on the vast extent of God's mercy towards us in Christ doesn't make our belief in Christ any less valuable. In fact, it calls us to draw closer to him, to take up his yoke that frees us from our burdens and invites us into the rest our souls desire. By clinging to Christ, by feeding on him in the worship and sacraments of the Church, we can come to him today, even now, and discover that by Grace he has already called us to himself, by his free gift, so that we dwell ever more in him, and he in us as we are opened to the transforming merciful judgement of the love of God.

Notes

1 Augustine, *Commentary on Psalm* 32.5, cited in von Balthasar, H., *Dare We Hope That All Men Be Saved: With A Short Discourse on Hell* (San Francisco: Ignatius Press, 1988), p. 116.

2 Exod. 34.6; Num. 14.18; Neh. 9.17; Pss 86.15; 103.8; 145.8; Joel 2.13; Jonah 4.2; cf. Nah. 1.3.

3 Faber, F., *Hymns* (London: Richardson & Son, 1862); cited in Arnold, R., *English Hymns of the Nineteenth Century: An Anthology* (New York: Peter Lang, 2004), pp. 124–5.

4 Pieper, J. 'On Hope', in *Faith, Hope, Love* (San Francisco: Ignatius Press, 1997), p. 128, cited in Balthasar, *Dare We Hope*, p. 123.

5 Pseudo-Clement, *Recognitions* 10.48, cited in Gavrilyuk, *The Suffering of the Impassible God*, p. 54.

6 See for example the recent reception of David Bentley Hart's defence of universal salvation in his *That All May Be Saved: Heaven, Hell and Universal Salvation* (London: Yale University Press, 2019).

7 Cf. Eph. 2.14.

8 Williams, R., 'The Finality of Christ', in *On Christian Theology* (Oxford: Blackwell, 2000), pp. 92–106, 104.

9 Pss 50.6; 75.7; cf. Acts 10.42.

10 Barth, K., 'The Proclamation of God's Free Grace', in *God Here and Now* (London: Routledge, 2003), pp. 34–54, 41–2.

11 See especially von Balthasar, *Dare We Hope*, pp. 18–31.

12 Von Balthasar, *Dare We Hope*, pp. 30–1.

13 Anselm, *Proslogion* 8–11; available at: stanselminstitute.org/files/AnselmProslogion.pdf (accessed 21.8.19).

14 Anselm, *Proslogion*, p. 8.

15 Anselm, *Proslogion*, pp. 9–11.

16 Anselm, *Proslogion*, p. 11; cf. von Balthasar, *Dare We Hope*, p. 118.

17 Aquinas, *Summa* 1.21.1–4; available at: www.newadvent.org/summa/1021.htm (accessed 20.8.19); von Balthasar, *Dare We Hope*, pp. 121–3.

18 Von Balthasar, *Dare We Hope*, p. 121. Aquinas cites Anselm, *Proslogion* 10, in *Summa* 1.21.1.

19 Aquinas echoes Anselm's argument from divine will in his reply to objection 2 at *Summa* 1.21.1.

20 McCabe, H., *On Aquinas* (London: Continuum, 2008), p. 150. There is a short discussion on justice with respect to human rights and the common good in Cuff, S., *Love in Action*, pp. 14–18.

21 Pseudo-Dionysius, *On the Divine Names* 8.4; Aquinas, *Summa* 1.21.1.

22 Aquinas, *Summa* 1.21.4.

23 Aquinas, *Summa* 1.21.4.

24 Pieper, 'Hope', p. 128.

25 Benedict XVI, *Spe Salvi* 1 (30 November 2007); available at w2.vatican.va/content/benedict-xvi/en/encyclicals/documents/hf_ben-xvi_enc_20071130_spe-salvi.html (accessed 20.8.19).

26 Benedict XVI, *Spe Salvi* 9

27 Faber, *Hymns*; cited in Arnold, *English Hymns*, p. 124.

28 Williams, 'Finality', p. 104.

29 Faber, *Hymns*; cited in Arnold, *English Hymns*, p. 124.

30 Faber, *Hymns*; cited in Arnold, *English Hymns*, p. 125.

31 Faber, *Hymns*; cited in Arnold, *English Hymns*, p. 125.

6

The Jealousy of God

His patience is indescribable, yet it exists as does His jealousy, His wrath, and any characteristic of this kind. But, if we conceive of these qualities, as they exist in us, He has none of them ... He is jealous without any ill will, as He is angry without being emotionally upset, as He pities without grieving, as He is sorry without correcting any fault; so He is patient without suffering at all. (St Augustine)[1]

'It's not fair.' We are born with an innate of sense of fairness. There is no way to annoy a child more than to frustrate this sense of fairness. We saw in the last chapter how one of the reasons discussion of the potential salvation of all people is so heated is that the idea of everyone being saved in Christ strikes at the heart of our instinctive notions of fairness; for anybody to get something for nothing. 'It's not fair'.

Moreover, we know that jealousy is a sin. In the Old Testament, we're instructed against jealousy: 'Thou shalt not covet thy neighbour's house, thou shalt not covet thy neighbour's wife, nor his manservant, nor his maidservant, nor his ox, nor his ass, nor any thing that is thy neighbour's' (Exod. 20.17). We're told not to be jealous.

And yet, our Old Testament also contains several difficult passages in which we read the opposite of God. Just verses before in Exodus we find: 'I the Lord your God am a jealous God, visiting the iniquity of the fathers upon the children to the third and the fourth generation of those who hate me'

(Exod. 20.5). We're not told not to be jealous. And yet God is. 'It's not fair.'

Christ and God's jealousy

What does it mean for God to be jealous? Is God as petulant as the child whose sense of fairness is violated, commanding one thing for us and doing quite a different thing himself? We could defend God from the charge of arbitrariness by asserting God's freedom. God is sovereign and free, if he wants to commend one course of action for us and take another himself, he's free to do so.

Sure enough, but before committing ourselves to saying that God can be arbitrary if he likes, we should first do what every piece of Christian thinking demands: begin and end with Christ. He is the Alpha and the Omega after all. God *is* free, but what that freedom looks like we only know through Christ. God reveals himself to us in Christ. He also reveals to us what it means to be human.

What then does God say to us in Christ? If God is jealous *of* us, his becoming one of us in Christ is a funny way of showing it. The Incarnation reminds us that whatever images and idols we make of god are not God. He comes to us, not the other way round. In fact, the Incarnation leads us to the startling realization that most of the images we have of God are idols, of our own or others' devising, which must constantly be checked against the true image of God shown to us in Christ.

We underestimate at our peril the difficulty of the task of making sure our images and ideas of God are being transformed and challenged by Christ. Ensuring that they are not idols of own making requires constant vigilance. Even the best ways of thinking and speaking about God can all too quickly become an idol, leading us to themselves and not to the God they once so clearly proclaimed to us. Even our worship can all too easily become idolatrous when *our worship* becomes the focus of our worship rather than the God we proclaim. Even the sacraments – those places where God has pledged his presence with us through water, bread and wine – can become idolatrous if *our celebration* of them becomes our focus rather than the God who pledges himself to us through them.

However, the task of ensuring that our images and ideas of God are not idols is easier said than done. For one thing, it feels dizzying and uncomfortable, and it's natural to respond by clinging ever more tightly to the image or idol of a god that has given us comfort or security in the past. Even here, Christ remains challenging us to ever sharpen our images and understanding of him, bringing them ever closer to the reality that is God. There's good reason to think this task will never be complete in our earthly lives. The idolatrous cobwebs on our understanding of God will only be fully blown away in eternity, when we see God face to face.

Idolatry

Given all this, what does it mean for God to be jealous? It's no coincidence that references to God's jealousy occur in discussion of the very idols we tend to make for ourselves: 'You shall not make for yourself an idol, whether in the form of anything that is in heaven above, or that is on the earth beneath, or that is in the water under the earth. You shall not bow down to them or worship them' (Exod. 20.4).

What is God jealous of? Not us, but those idols and images of gods and even God that we make for ourselves. And not just for ourselves but for others too. Humankind's ability to make idols is so pervasive that we're reminded that the consequences of such idol-making are huge. Not only do we worship the idols of *our* making, we're all too ready to worship the idols devised by others too. Every sort of idolatry is contagious, which is why it's such a serious matter.

We might think idolatry is a minority interest or a concern of the ancient past. Very few of us have made an image of a little deity to put on our desk or have a sacred pole in our garden or window box that we worship in the place of God. However, idolatry runs deeper than this. How many of us begin our day by rushing to our phones or computers? How many of our lives are ordered not around the liturgical year but the fixtures calendar or the release date of the next series of our favourite show? How many of us truly and constantly put God at the centre of our focus and build our life from that centre? How many of the things that we have and do every day are actually those on which we want to build our lives?

Our tendency to idolatry runs so deep that we're told we have to go to rather extraordinary lengths to try to keep our attention focused on God. Stephen Fowl notes

> the Old Testament's unrelenting insistence on the singular-ity of God (most decisively stated in Deuteronomy 6). There is only one God who calls forth our whole-hearted, single-minded love and worship. Nothing else can be allowed to divert us from our love and worship of God. This is why scripture contains such a strong polemic against 'idols'.[2]

Deuteronomy 6 is key, according to Fowl, in demonstrating the need to develop the kind of concrete practices that elimin-ate the potential for idolatry.[3] At Deuteronomy 6.4-5 we find the *Shema*: 'Hear, O Israel: The Lord is our God, the Lord alone. You shall love the Lord your God with all your heart, and with all your soul, and with all your might.'[4] Deuteron-omy 6 is clear that it is not enough just to know and believe in these words. They are followed by the command to 'recite them to your children and talk about them when you are at home and when you are away, when you lie down and when you rise' (Deut. 6.7). The Shema is not only to be said but reflected upon and talked about throughout one's life and at key points during the day. Fowl notes that these verses demonstrate the requirements for catechesis – teaching about the faith.[5] The aim of catechesis is to prevent the words from becoming an idol. Catechesis attempts to teach those who receive the words of the Shema not to separate them from the divine reality to which they point.

Deuteronomy 6.6–7 strongly suggests that this catechesis must be intentional and constant. In order to prevent the risk of idolatry, the Israelites are called to catechize their children, to teach the faith to generation after generation. They are not just called to teach the words of the Shema to them. They are to teach the words of the Shema wherever they go, every day. Moreover, Deuteronomy 6.8–9 records the lengths that the Israelites must go to keep these words at the forefront of their minds. They must display them everywhere: 'Bind them as a sign on your hand, fix them as an emblem on your forehead, and write them on the doorposts of your house and on your gates.' The danger of idolatry is ever-present.[6] The lengths to which Deuteronomy 6 goes to in order to teach the Israelites to keep the words of the Shema at the forefront of their lives indicates the ever-constant risk of falling away from true worship into idolatry.

Fowl notes that the slip into idolatry is incremental and rarely intentional. Most of the time that we are engaged in idolatry, we are completely unaware that this is what we are doing. To prevent sliding into idolatry requires constant catechesis and, Fowl argues, the development of public practices to demonstrate our allegiance to God and to guard against the slip into idolatry.[7] This is therefore a communal practice of catechesis and profession of faith. However, Fowl notes that even the content of our catechesis and symbols of public profession of faith can all too quickly become idols if detached from their catechetical foundation.[8] To avoid the slip into idolatry requires constant intentionality as to how and what we are worshipping, how we are speaking and thinking about God, and whether even the words and devices that were once vehicles of true worship have become idolatrous ciphers disconnected from the teaching and community of faith.

Worship and Idolatry

Making sure that our communal teaching and practice of the faith is not slipping into idolatry is likewise easier said than done. We tend to favour a teaching and worship style that fits our preferences. We find it hard to listen to teaching that challenges us or to find God in ways of worship that we don't like. We check church websites and noticeboards for signs that we would like or dislike worshipping there, rather than expecting that we might meet God there whatever the teaching or worship is like. As Christian communities, it's all too easy to become communities that worship this or that particular teaching, even if it is biblical, rather than God. It's all too easy to become communities that worship this or that way of worshipping, even if the presence of God was once at the heart of the means of worship transmitted to us by our mothers and fathers in the faith.

One of the most painful realizations about idolatry and the Christian faith is that even the most sacred means of Christian encounter do not escape our propensity for idolatry. Teaching and practices that can become means of divine encounter can also become means of idolatrous distraction. The danger here is great, as it is in these places of potential sacred encounter that we find it most difficult to spot where idolatry has crept in. Are we worshipping God or our particular way of reading and interpreting the Bible? Are we worshipping God or our particular way of living the Christian life? Are we worshipping God or our particular style of worship, our particular way of celebrating the sacraments of God's Church? Ensuring that God is the real object of our worship is a perennial task.

It's important here to recognize the role of the sacraments of the Church as a means of safeguarding us from the ever-present risk of idolatry. It is the case, as we have already noted, that *our* particular way of celebrating the sacraments can become an idol. However, the sacraments themselves offer us the best kind of catechetical communal practice of the sort

Fowl recognizes as vital in preventing the slippage into idolatry as a community of faith.[9]

Baptism – God's use of water as an act of initiation into his Church. Eucharist – God's use of bread and wine to be present in our midst and to build up the body of Christ. The sacraments are God's gift of material in creation through which to focus our worship, to prevent us from focusing our worship on some other aspect of creation and creating an idol of our own. The sacraments don't require us to stop our tendency to fix on aspects of the material creation. They are God's presence within material creation, which means we meet him in worship when we do.

Moreover, if we don't unite around the sacraments that Christ has given us, there is a danger that we make sacramental idols of our own. If we don't celebrate the sacraments of the Church, we all too quickly end up celebrating other sacraments of our own devising: the vestments, or the use of technology, the worship band or the organ, the individual testimony or the communion antiphon.

The sacraments help us avoid idolatry in another way too. As places of God's activity and presence in the world, the sacraments train us to look for God's Spirit at work elsewhere in creation – or they should. All too easily even the sacraments become an idol if we start seeing God's presence and activity in these moments alone. If we become so fixated on them that we fail to recognize that they help us to see more of God's work in the world, not less.

The Jealousy of God

We might still ask: why is God, the creator of the universe, of all that is, jealous of these trifling and meaningless idols that we make for ourselves? Why be *jealous* of false deities or mobile phones when you've rather bigger things to contemplate as the all-powerful and all-knowing? Why is he bothered if we become a little too fixated on the words or practices designed to aid our worship rather than on him as the object of our worship?

The jealousy of God isn't God's jealousy *of* us. He isn't really jealous of the multiplicity of our idols and our constant habit of making idols out of anything and everything we encounter. Rather, God's jealousy is his jealousy *for* us. God knows how easily we worship idols of our own devising and he knows how costly such worship can be. He knows that lives lived in relationship with him, lives lived with him truly at their centre, are the only lives that are really true and full and free. He knows this because he created us, and because he knows the abundance of that life he wants us to enjoy with him – life in all its fullness (John 10.10).

God is jealous *for* us because he wants us to live that life today. And he isn't just jealous for *some* of us, he doesn't just want *some* people to live that life today – just Jews or just Greeks or just men or just women – he wants us all to live that life even now.[10]

God is jealous because he wants us to put him at the centre of our lives. He wants us to do that for which we were created, to live our lives in relationship with him – lives shot through with that self-emptying love that is our very God himself: Father, Son, and Holy Spirit. He wants us to empty ourselves of the false images and idols of our own devising and take up our true selves – the lives he longs us to live.

Is this fair? Not a bit. God's jealousy, like God's love, is utterly indiscriminate, utterly unearned by anything we can do, utterly gracious, and utterly gift. Fair? No. But worth being jealous of? Absolutely. Those of us not living that life as fully as we might – which is all of us – should cultivate a little bit more divine jealousy, and be jealous of those living more of that life than us today, jealous for that life in all its fullness, which only love brings.

Notes

1 Augustine, *On Patience* 1.1; available at: www.newadvent.org/
fathers/1315.htm (accessed 17.8.19).

2 Fowl, S. E., 'What scripture does and does not say on God', in
The Church Times (12 February 2016); available at www.churchtimes.
co.uk/articles/2016/12-february/features/features/scripture-and-the-
doctrine-of-god (accessed 20.8.19). See further Fowl, S. E., *Idolatry*
(Waco, TX: Baylor University Press, 2019).

3 Fowl, S. E., 'How To Eat Until We Are Full: Idolatry and Ways
To Avoid It' (Lecture given at Seattle Pacific University 22 January
2015 and St Mellitus College 4 March 2019); available at: www.you-
tube.com/watch?v=E50Ro9xrCvQ (accessed 20.8.19).

4 Wood, W., *Analytic Theology and the Academic Study of Religion* (Oxford: Oxford University Press, 2020) also begins his chapter
on idolatry with reflection on the Shema and the emphasis on God's
worthiness for worship by creation arising out of his being Creator. Bill
Wood kindly let me read this chapter ahead of publication. The end of
his chapter explores the role of the Creator/creature distinction we have
been exploring and the accusation of idolatry made against those who
do not hold to the classical view of God's attributes and perfections.

5 Fowl, 'How To Eat'.

6 Wood, *Analytic*, notes the nature of idolatry as a perennial human
temptation requiring theologians of every age to critique it.

7 Fowl, 'How To Eat'.

8 Fowl, 'How To Eat'.

9 Fowl, 'How To Eat'.

10 Cf. 1 Tim. 2.4.

7

Prayer

Prayer is the light of the soul, giving us true knowledge of God. It is a link mediating between God and man. By prayer the soul is borne up to heaven and in a marvellous way embraces the Lord. This meeting is like that of an infant crying on its mother, and seeking the best of milk. The soul longs for its own needs and what it receives is better than anything to be seen in the world. Prayer is a precious way of communicating with God, it gladdens the soul and gives repose to its affections. You should not think of prayer as being a matter of words. It is a desire for God, an indescribable devotion, not of human origin, but the gift of God's grace. (From a homily attributed to St John Chrysostom)[1]

In Luke's Gospel one of the disciples makes one of the most important requests of Jesus in the whole of our gospels: 'Lord, teach us to pray' (Luke 11.1). This is a question we should always be asking of God. If nothing else, asking this question of God is the foundation of a healthy prayer life. If we're honest, all our prayer lives are terrible. We get distracted. Our mind wanders. We do not pray as we think we ought. If we're struggling to pray, we can do little better than ask, 'Lord, teach us to pray'.

However, this request isn't only for those new to prayer, or those of us whose prayer life has grown stale. In our last chapter we traced the dangers of idolatry. The dangers of idolatry are an ever-present risk in our prayer lives too. Even our prayers and ways of praying are open to the risk of becoming idols. How do we avoid this? 'Lord, teach us to pray' is an ever-useful prayer to pray in order to help lessen the perennial risk of worshipping our way of worshipping.

This chapter seeks to explore the phenomenon of prayer to the God of classical theism: the God who is omniscient, omnipotent and benevolent. Put more simply, the paradox of praying to the God who knows everything, can do anything, and is good and wants the best for us. In this chapter we ask how much of our prayer actually reflects our understanding of the God to whom we know we are praying. How and why is it that God wants us to pray at all? What might our prayer lives look like if God were really front and centre, the focus of our prayers?

Prayer as Dialogue

Most of us begin our prayers with a list of requests. We list all the things that we'd like God to do for us, or that we want to happen in our lives. 'Please get me that job.' 'Please help me with this.' 'Please cure this person.' 'Please stop that war.' All too often we make our request and then get up from our pew or leave our home group and switch our mind to something else.

Prayer is a dialogue. It is an invitation to address God, and to wait. We so often skip this step – to wait to let ourselves be addressed by him. It's as if we phone up a friend, blurt out everything we want, and hang up before our friend has a chance to respond. When we pray, it is of course much more difficult to wait and to listen. It is much easier to make our prayer lives a series of holy shopping lists by directing prayers at God. It is much harder to open ourselves to being directed by him.

Prayer may begin with our prayer requests but it doesn't end there. We have to give God a chance to respond, and then spend some time with him. This is where the more difficult and rewarding business of praying begins.

This aspect of prayer is often the most intimidating. The ease with which we can pray a list of requests in contrast to the more difficult task of waiting and listening means that we can often get demoralized and give up on this deeper kind of prayer entirely. Despite our best intentions, some other holy task always seems more important or worthwhile or more likely to get results. When we're tempted to put some other task in the ways of this waiting and listening, we should recall Christ's praise of Mary for sitting at his feet and listening, while Martha is distracted with the many tasks of ministry (Luke 10.38–42).

If this seems daunting, Rowan Williams offers us an image of such prayer which helps us here. He compares prayer to sunbathing:

> When you're lying on the beach or under the lamp, something is happening, something that has nothing to do with how you feel or how hard you're trying. You're not going to get a better tan by screwing up your eyes and concentrating. You give the time, and that's it. All you have to do is turn up. And then things change, at their own pace. You simply have to be there where the light can get at you ... Give the time and let go of trying hard (actually this is the difficult bit). God is there always. You don't need to fight for his attention or make yourself acceptable. He's glad to see you. And he'll make a difference while you're not watching, just by radiating who and what he is in your direction. All he asks is that you stay there with him for a while, in the light. For the rest, you just trust him to get on with it.[2]

If we allow ourselves to wait and to listen our prayer life can develop from a one-sided phone call to an intimate communion between yourself and God. The rest of this chapter explores what God might be doing in prayer, and what he asks us to do in response.

Prayer is a dialogue with God as we stay and wait with him a while. As in any dialogue there are two conversation partners.

This means that prayer demands awareness of God, but also awareness of ourselves.

Awareness of God

Prayer requires awareness of ourselves, but it also requires awareness of the other conversation partner who makes up the intimate dialogue of prayer. Our exploration of the God of classical theism has attempted to increase our awareness of the Christian doctrine of God.

The God to whom we pray is not a different God from the God who created us and whom we worship. Yet often our prayers seem to forget the attributes of God that we take for granted in the rest of our Christian lives. In the rest of our lives we acknowledge God's omniscience. We recognize his perfect knowledge. We believe that God has searched us out and known us, he knows when we sit down and rise, he discerns our thoughts from afar, before a word is on our tongue, he knows it completely (Psalm 139.1–4). We acknowledge God's omnipotence. We believe that for him all things are possible. We recognize God's benevolence. We know he wants good for us. We know that ultimately he wills our salvation to eternal life.

Yet, when it comes to our prayer lives, the concept of God presupposed in our prayers bear little resemblance to the omnipotent, omniscient and benevolent God in whom we believe. We often waste time in prayer by neglecting what we believe to be true about God in the rest of our Christian lives. We can waste time by telling God something he already knows: 'Dear God, we read in the news today about this difficult situation.' We can waste time by asking him to do things that he is already doing: 'Dear God, please do the best for me.' We can waste time by asking him to do things he will never do: 'Dear God, I don't care if this isn't going to be good for me in the long run, but I really really want that job, so please let me get it.'

If we neglect the nature of God in our prayers, we can spend so much time telling things God he knows, or asking him to do things he's already doing, or asking him to do things he will never do, that we don't actually get down to the more difficult work of praying.

This might make us think: if God knows everything or everything it is possible to know (he is omniscient), and God has the power to do anything or anything it is possible to do (omnipotent), and God is good and wants what is best for us, why should we pray at all?

Why should we pray? Why pray to a God who knows everything, can do anything, and is always doing good for us? For a start, prayer is assumed throughout the Gospels and the Bible as whole. In fact, prayer is not just assumed but we're encouraged to pray: 'Love your enemies and pray for those who persecute you' (Matt. 5.44). In Luke's Gospel, Jesus tells his disciples 'a parable to the effect that they ought always to pray and not lose heart' (Luke 18.1). Not only are we told to pray, but to pray always.

Moreover, if we seek to follow the pattern of Christ, Christ himself prays. We read in the letter to the Hebrews: 'during the days of Jesus' life, he offered up prayers and petitions' (Heb. 5.7). We see this again and again on the pages of our Gospels. Jesus takes time to pray: 'During those days he went out to the mountain to pray; and he spent the night in prayer to God' (Luke 6.12). It is clear throughout the pages of Scripture and the Gospels that we are meant to pray.

And yet our prayer remains prayer to the omniscient, omnipotent and benevolent God, which ever gives rise to the question: 'Why pray at all?' This means that our prayer is not what it might at first seem. Being told to pray to a God who knows everything, has the power to do anything and is always good means that prayer is not a way to get what we want, nor a way to tell God something he doesn't know, nor to get him to do something he can't otherwise do or is already doing.

Instead, because God knows everything, God has the power to do anything and God is good, our prayer takes on a different character from our instinctive sense of prayer as simply a list of requests and things for which we want to ask. If we are called to pray to an omniscient, omnipotent and benevolent God, and our prayer is meaningful, then praying to an omniscient, omnipotent, benevolent God means that prayer is a way by which God has decided to achieve certain things. We pray because our prayers are 'efficacious'. They really work, they *do* something. Our prayer is a means that God has decided to use to do whatever he has decided to do by way of those prayers.

As such, God is not only the recipient of prayer, but also its source. God puts prayers into our hearts. The Spirit himself intercedes for us: 'the Spirit helps us in our weakness; for we do not know how to pray as we ought, but that very Spirit intercedes with sighs too deep for words' (Rom. 8.24).

Most of all, this means that prayer is gratuitous. Prayer is an extravagant, exuberant, over-the-top gift that God has granted us. Prayer is a privileged opportunity to commune, to converse, to strengthen our relationship with God. Prayer is extravagant because prayer isn't needed for God to achieve his will (because he is all-powerful, all-knowing, and all-good). Viewed this way, prayer is no different from the Christian life as a whole. Prayer, like Grace, is not deserved but freely given.

This means that our focus moves from 'Why pray?' to 'How to pray?' and 'What to pray?' While answers to the question 'How to pray?' are as many as the number of Christian traditions of prayer, we will consider a few basic requirements of almost all traditions of prayer when we think of how we might be aware of ourselves as the other conversation partner in the gratuitous communion that is prayer.

When prayer is viewed in this way, the question 'What to pray?' takes on a special importance. What are we called to pray for so that our prayer becomes the means of achieving God's will that God desires it to be? Why is it that God is putting this prayer in my heart? Am I really praying the prayers that God wants me to pray? What should I pray?

We need to be reflective in our prayers, both in what we

are praying and how God is making use of our prayers. This requires the gift of discernment. Reflecting on what and why we pray makes us better *pray*-ers as our wills become ever more aligned to his.

However, caution is needed here. If the thought of all these questions is making you anxious even thinking about praying, our reflection on what we are to pray can't be another task we put in the way of spending time in prayer. As Williams reminded us, 'all you have to do is turn up. And then things change, at their own pace.'[3] Praying is often the best form of reflection on prayer. Putting ourselves where the light can get us, and trusting that God will do the rest.

Discernment

We've considered what it might mean to be aware of God in our prayers. We will shortly consider what it means for us to be aware of ourselves in prayer. However, given the responsibility for us to pray the prayers that God is willing us to pray, we should first reflect on the importance of discernment in the life of prayer.

There is not space here to unpack fully the concept of discernment within the Christian life. To be able to articulate any notion of discernment requires sustained engagement with the Christian life that is well beyond the spiritual capabilities of the author of this book. The thoughts below reflect some of the basic contours of Christian discernment. However, we should first note that of all the Christian traditions of prayer, the one that has done most reflecting on the place of discernment is the Ignatian tradition of prayer stemming from St Ignatius of Loyola (1491–1556), which is at the heart of the Jesuit order.

Ignatius's *Spiritual Exercises* contain two sets of rules for spiritual discernment.[4] At their heart, these rules for discernment reminds us of the importance of vigilance and attention in discernment, and warn us from moving too quickly from what pleases us to identifying that with God's will. As we shall see, a certain amount of hesitancy and provisionality is a key feature of Christian discernment.

Sandra Schneiders defines discernment as 'the ability to see the revelatory meaning in the ongoing process of one's own or another's life; to see, as the saints say, "with the eyes of faith" the salvific significance of what seem to be ordinary events'.[5] Schneiders' definition offers us an important insight into the nature of discernment. Discernment isn't our openness to the miraculous, but the ability to see God in the everyday and in the course of our daily lives.

Stanley Hauerwas likewise focuses on the everyday over the miraculous as the arena of discernment. He is suspicious of focusing too much on miraculous experiences in the Christian life because they can lead us astray and encourage us 'to catch rather than be caught by the Holy Spirit'.[6] Hauerwas demonstrates one important feature of Christian discernment in this article. He is hesitant to assume too quickly that this or that is the work of God. This shows in his hesitancy to claim the Holy Spirit as being on his side: 'I do not want to give the impression that the Holy Spirit is on my side. That does not mean I think the Holy Spirit does not have a side, I am just unsure I get to claim that side as my side.'[7]

Discernment involves a reflection on God in the course of our daily lives, and demands a certain amount of reluctance to jump too quickly to presuming that God is on our side. Peter de Villiers highlights the importance of the wider Christian community in the task of discernment. Discerning how and what to pray is never a task we can do alone, but always as part of the wider body of Christ. It is for this reason that the daily office of morning and evening prayer is such a vital part of any prayer life. The communal praying of the office, and particularly the recitation of the psalms, with all those praying the office wherever they may be in the world, means that the daily office is a key building block in such prayerful discernment. When we pray the daily office of morning and evening prayer, we are reminded that we never pray alone, and our discernment is always communal.

De Villiers takes the account of the gathering in Acts 15 as a paradigm for such Christian discernment. Acts 15 includes the account of the meeting of apostles and elders to decide whether Gentile converts to Christianity need to keep the whole of the Jewish law. De Villiers notes that this gathering

> aims at deeper understanding by drawing on the insight of those who are more experienced. They include those with seniority, not only in terms of knowledge, but also in terms of maturity. This maturity is characterized by integrity, by a willingness to share and an openness to listen carefully, but is, most of all, driven by a sense of unity and belonging. It also involves openness on the part of those who speak and those who are heard, to submit themselves to the scrutiny of those who accompany them on their spiritual journey.[8]

Discernment is a communal activity but also one that recognizes the experience and maturity of those who have wisdom to offer in deciding how and what to pray. Crucially, de Villiers also alerts us to the work of God in prompting our discernment. As we noted above, God puts prayers into our hearts. De Villiers points to this collaboration of human and divine as key to the model of discernment given in Acts 15. He notes that in Acts 15.28 the phrase included in the Apostles' letter indicating the result of their discernment ('it has seemed good to the Holy Spirit and to us') mentions 'the Holy Spirit first and before the expression "and us" heightens awareness of the role of the divine ... so that their decision is also a decision of the Holy Spirit'.[9] If we discern the work of the Holy Spirit and open ourselves to being caught by that same Spirit, Hauerwas and de Villiers remind us of the need for hesitance in presuming God is on our side of a debate, the insight of the wider Christian community, and the wisdom and maturity of those experienced in discerning in faith.

Awareness of Ourselves

Prayer requires an awareness of the God to whom we pray and a commitment to discernment in how we pray, but also an awareness of ourselves as those who are called to pray. Awareness of ourselves means being attentive to our mood and our surroundings as we attempt to pray. It's no good trying to settle down to half an hour of prayer if you're in a doctor's waiting room and expect to be called any minute, or you're completely exhausted and can barely open your eyes. Awareness of ourselves also means we need to be aware of common patterns that we can fall into as human beings and common obstacles that we can put between ourselves and God.

Throughout this book, we have attempted to draw out some common obstacles in our instinctive responses of which we need to be aware whenever we begin the dialogue of prayer. These include our tendency to make idols for ourselves, our frustration when our sense of fairness is disturbed, our habit of participating in the relentless logic of tribalism to build walls around our group and to judge who is in and who is out. These are just some of the barriers to prayer and the Christian life that we erect for ourselves.

Awareness of ourselves reminds us that prayer requires our vigilance in the face of such pitfalls. The best way to be vigilant is, in Williams' words, to put ourselves where the light can get us, to give God the time and trust that he will get on with tearing down all those barriers we place between ourselves and him.

In practical terms, there are some very basic steps we can take to help us become aware of ourselves as we begin to develop in the life of prayer. Preparation is key. We need to set aside time to pray, and know how long we are going to pray for. It's no use spending most of our time *just* staring at our watch. We need to be purposeful. Prayer requires our attention, especially time spent in silent prayer. We need to be intentional about giving this or that amount of time to God.

Most of our time spent in silence will be time spent trying to be silent. We acknowledge all the thoughts that creep in and continue to give the time we've set aside to God. Prayer is like exercise, it takes time and repetition and requires practice. To use Williams' image, the more time we open ourselves to the light of God in prayer, the better our spiritual tan will be.

Awareness of ourselves also means we need to be aware of our past and present. What has gone or is going on in our lives will affect what we pray. We can ask: 'How are our prayers being affected by our lives? Are the prayers that immediately spring to mind that for which God is really asking us to pray?' We also need to be aware of ourselves in a simply physical sense. Prayer requires that we are aware of our bodies. We need to notice whether we're comfortable or distracted. All of these impact our ability to pray.

Finally, we need to pay attention to the words we use in prayer. What phrases do we use again and again? What do they mean? What are our constant prayers that we pray over and over again? What new prayer might God be putting on our lips? Reflecting on these habits of prayer, as part of developing an awareness of ourselves in prayer, will help us develop in the life of prayer, and pray those prayers that God is willing us to pray.

However, prayer requires more than words. Graham Ward describes this well, in a passage worth quoting at length to conclude our discussion of prayer in the light of God's being:

> Prayer is not just intercession, and prayer need not be vocalized at all. Being in the world in Christ, being in the world as Christ, as a living organism, we are continually being called on to respond to the environment that envelops us. We respond physically, emotionally, and mentally. Indeed, we cannot apprehend all the levels on which we are responding … There is prayer at conscious, verbalized levels – public prayer, the solitary confession, thanksgiving, the Ave (Hail Mary) or Our Father, for example. But dwelling as we are in

Christ, there is praying at somatic (bodily) and mental levels over which we have no control. There is praying that goes on within us as the Spirit breathes and the soul communes. The world's events as they come to our attention from various sources – the media, present circumstances, the hearing of other people's stories, and so forth – are filtered through our ensouled flesh. They are registered within and they modify within as we attune ourselves to the world. That miraculous escape we read about in the newspaper that caused us joy, those gangs of teenage girls and boys congregating at the corner shop late at night that cause us to fear and move us to pity, those scenes of carnage on the news in the wake of a bomb attack that cause us to shudder at the violence and grieve with the shell-shocked – all these events pass through us and change us. And as we dwell in Christ and Christ in us, then they pass through Christ also. This is what I mean by praying: that deep inhabitation of the world, its flesh and its spirit, that stirs a contemplation and a reading of the signs of the times that is more profound than we can ever apprehend or appreciate.[10]

Prayer is more than words. Prayer is more than silence. Just like the love of God we explored above, prayer requires the whole of ourselves. Prayer has the potential to be our entire lives, or perhaps better, our entire lives have the potential to become prayer. The more we pray, the more we offer ourselves. The heart of prayer is this self-offering. God offers himself to us, inviting us into the dialogue of prayer, and we are invited to offer ourselves to him. And as we do so, we find the mystery at the heart of the Christian life, the mystery of the nature of love. The more we respond to God's offering to us, the more we offer ourselves to him and those around us, the more we find the true selves that God is ever inviting us to become.

What our offering might look like depends on the prayer that God puts in our heart. Here we see why the awareness of God is so important and why a focus on discernment of what it is that God is calling us to is a vital part of the life of prayer. What that offering will look like also depends on the contexts within and to which we are called, the needs of those around us and the requirements of justice wherever we find ourselves. We now turn ourselves to this task as we conclude by thinking about what kind of action God might be calling us to, given who and how he has revealed himself to be.

Notes

1 Sacred Congregation for Divine Worship, *The Divine Office Volume II: Daily Prayer for Lent and Eastertide* (London: Collins, 2006), pp. 21–2 (from the second reading of the Office of Readings appointed on the Friday following Ash Wednesday).

2 Williams, R. 'Pause for Thought' on the Terry Wogan Show, BBC Radio 2 (18th October 2005); available at https://chpublishing.co.uk/media/74571/life-source-extras.pdf (accessed 20.8.19).

3 Williams, 'Pause'.

4 Ganns, G. (trans.), *The Spiritual Exercises of Saint Ignatius: A Translation and Commentary* (Chicago, IL: Loyola University Press, 1992). The *Exercises* are a quite formidable text. Martin, J., *The Jesuit Guide to Almost Everything: A Spirituality for Real Life* (New York: Harper Collins, 2012) is an accessible starting point, especially pp. 305–38 on discernment. I owe Fr Ben Kerridge a debt of thanks for his wisdom in conversation on discernment in the Ignatian tradition.

5 Schneiders, S. M., 'Spiritual discernment in the Dialogue of Saint Catherine of Siena', in *Horizons* 9 (1982), pp. 47–59, 49; cited in de Villiers, P. G. R., 'Communal Discernment in the Early Church', in *Acta Theologica* 17 (2013), pp. 132–55, 132.

6 Hauerwas, S., 'How to be Caught by the Holy Spirit' (14 November 2013); available at: www.abc.net.au/religion/how-to-be-caught-by-the-holy-spirit/10099524 (accessed 20.8.19).

7 Hauerwas, 'Caught'.

8 De Villiers, 'Communal', pp. 141–2.

9 De Villiers, 'Communal', p. 149.

10 Ward, G., *The Politics of Discipleship: Becoming Postmaterial Citizens* (Grand Rapids, MI: Baker Academic, 2009), pp. 281–2.

8

The God of Life

There was a time when the Church was very powerful. It was during that period when the early Christians rejoiced when they were deemed worthy to suffer for what they believed. In those days the Church was not merely a thermometer that recorded the ideas and principles of popular opinion; it was a thermostat that transformed the mores of society. Wherever the early Christians entered a town the power structure got disturbed. (Martin Luther King)[1]

Our exploration of the God of classical theism as the source and summit of inspiration for living the Christian life is almost complete. In this chapter we summarize the results of our discussion and ask what it means to act as creatures in the world in line with what we know about the Creator of that world. As God's creation, how do we live in the way our Creator intends? How do we snap out of our old and instinctive ways of existing within the created order and live as that new creation which God is ever calling us to be?[2]

God and Us

To be aware of the God of classical theism is to relinquish the notion that *our* ways of existing are the summit of what it means to be. As we saw in our exploration of divine simplicity, whatever it means to be created, God transcends as Creator. This is an affront to our human desire for power and control.

We are ever trying to usurp the transcendence of God in our action, in our relations with each other, in the way we describe the world to be. We are ever trying to build our own towers of Babel to elevate ourselves above not only God, but those fellow creatures around us, other human beings over whom we long to be transcendent and to control.

Awareness of God shatters all these pretensions we have to make ourselves 'god'. Moltmann is correct when he says:

> To know God in the cross of Christ is a crucifying form of knowledge, because it shatters everything to which a man can hold and on which he can build, both his works and his knowledge of reality, and precisely in so doing sets him free.[3]

It is not only the cross of Christ that liberates us from the constraints of our knowledge. As we reflect on the nature of God this too liberates us from the limitations of our creaturely perspective. It is precisely because of God's transcendence to us as creation that we realize the limits of our human ways of being. We come to realize the futility of our desire to hoard power and wealth for ourselves.

Reflecting on divine simplicity leads us to a position of humility. Each and every one of us is created in God's image (Gen. 1.26–8). And yet all too easily we forget that this is not a licence to act as we please in relation to the world around us. We mistake 'dominion' for 'domination'. We neglect to think through the consequences of what this means for acting in relation to our fellow human beings. We relish acting in the image of God, while neglecting to recognize the image of God in those around us.[4] We mistake our creation in God's image for our creation as 'God'.

The irony here is that the 'god' in whose image we desire to act bears no resemblance to the God who has revealed himself to us. The 'god' whose position we try to usurp is a 'god' of human longing – the longing for power, the longing for control, the longing for self. If we were truly to act in the image of the Christian God, if we were truly to usurp his place, it would not be by elevating ourselves over and above our fellow human beings and the rest of creation. It would not be by seeking power and control and fulfilment of our own selfish longings and desires:

> Do nothing from selfish ambition or conceit, but in humility regard others as better than yourselves. Let each of you look not to your own interests, but to the interests of others. Let the same mind be in you that was in Christ Jesus, who, though he was in the form of God, did not regard equality with God as something to be exploited, but emptied himself, taking the form of a slave, being born in human likeness. And being found in human form, he humbled himself and became obedient to the point of death – even death on a cross. (Phil 2.3–8)

If we want two images of the nature of God, St Paul sets them clearly before us: the crib and the cross. A helpless infant, and an innocent victim. The Christian God is not the god of our own imaginings, but the God who pours himself out completely, whose very nature is the eternal mutual outpouring of love in the Godhead: Father, Son and Holy Spirit.

Reflecting on the transcendence of God as creator, which is at the heart of the doctrine of divine simplicity, puts into stark relief the emptiness of the images of 'god' and the many 'gods' we create for ourselves. Nowhere is God more alien or transcendent to our creaturely expectations of deity than when he is born as one of us, a helpless babe who grows to be a tortured innocent executed as a criminal. The irony is rich here. In this very transcendence, he is intimately immanent. He is one of us. In revealing his transcendence as God to us, he reveals to us our real selves – the true selves he is calling us to be. He teaches us how to act in the world, to be fully human, to enjoy that gift of life in all its fullness for which we long.

The task of learning how to receive this gift lasts a lifetime.

In fact, none of us ever learn how to receive it completely. We always try to cling to this or that bit of ourselves. As we saw in our exploration of God's jealousy, we are forever clinging to idols of our own making, even making idols of the ways that helped us receive this gift of life in the past. We struggle, through sin, to fully give ourselves in the way that God has given himself to us and continues to give himself to us. We struggle to live those lives of constant self-gift which we saw was what it meant to love.

As we struggle, as we cling to ourselves or our idols, as we give up trying to live the life of self-gift altogether we mar the image of God in those around us. We neglect to treat our fellow human beings as created in the image of God. Our love for God and for neighbour fails. Or, more likely, we're simply indifferent. We become hardened and indifferent to the pain and suffering our actions cause, the cost of the convenience of our lifestyle, or we miss the one crying out in need on our very doorstep. We find ourselves

> afraid of the destructive creative power of love. We need and deeply want to be loved and to love, and yet when that happens it seems a threat, because we are asked to give ourselves up, to abandon our selves; and so when we meet love we kill it.[5]

We get caught up in cycles of suffering and despair, and we perpetuate the very suffering from which Christ came to redeem us.

This is true not only for us as individuals, but for the Church as a whole. Moltmann notes that 'the memory of the passion and resurrection of Christ is as the same time both dangerous and liberating. It endangers a church which is adapted to the religious politics of its time and brings it into fellowship with the sufferers of its time.'[6] The Church is ever in danger of idolizing and aligning itself to the politics and mores of the present or an idolized past.

The Challenge of God

If the Church is to be become the 'thermostat' that transforms the mores of society, to use Martin Luther King's image, then reflecting on the nature of God is key. Moltmann is right when he argues that:

> the Christian church and Christian theology become relevant to the problems of the modern world only when they reveal the 'hard core' of their identity in the crucified Christ and through it are called into question, together with the society in which they live ... Faith, the church and theology must demonstrate what they really believe and hope about the man from Nazareth who was crucified under Pontius Pilate, and what practical consequences they wish to draw from this. The crucified Christ himself is a challenge to Christian theology and the Christian church, which dare to call themselves by his name.[7]

In our exploration of God's relationship to suffering, we saw how Moltmann's own account of the 'hard core' of our identity suffered from an inadequate account of God's redemptive transformation of human suffering. However, he is right in pointing our attention to the need to reveal the 'hard core' of Christian identity to the world in order to call into question the societies in which we live and our own contribution to those societies. The 'hard core' of our Christian faith is a challenge to every unjust status quo: 'wherever the early Christians entered a town the power structure got disturbed'.[8]

Moreover, it is essential to the Christian challenge to society that we point not only to Christ as the man from Nazareth, but to Christ as the man whose life and death God lived and died, through which God transformed the very nature of life and death. It is not just the crucifixion that challenges Christian theology, the Church, and all who dare call themselves by his name, but the whole of God's life with us: his birth, his death, his Risen life today. Moreover, it is not just the nature of the humanity that God takes to himself that has practical consequences for us, but the nature of the God who takes humanity to himself and the potential for human life he reveals in doing so.

What are those practical consequences? In this book we have traced some aspects of the nature of God according to classical theism. We defended the doctrine of the simplicity of God as affirming the distinction between us as creatures and God as Creator. We saw the fruits of that doctrine in the identity of attributes which mean that what appear to be contradictory attributes in human beings, or according to our way of thinking, are in fact united in God. We saw how this helped us to understand some attributes of God by illuminating them in relation to other attributes. This exploration of God has also revealed to us a pattern for the Christian life that helps us to live the human life revealed to us in Christ.

In his relationship to suffering, we argued that God doesn't suffer suffering, he transforms it. Likewise, as Christians we aren't called simply to *acknowledge* the suffering and pain around us. We are called to *do* something, to seek to transform the situations of pain and suffering. To alleviate pain where we can, to prevent situations of suffering, to break open the cycles of misery and death that lead to the pain and suffering of those around us.

In considering God's love, we saw what it meant for God to be love. To love means to pour ourselves out as God poured himself out for us in Christ, as Christ poured himself out for us on the cross, as the Father pours himself out to the Son and Spirit, as the Son pours himself out to Spirit and Father, as Spirit pours himself out to Father and Son. Love requires the whole of ourselves. There is not one bit of us that is not called upon to be taken up in love.

The mystery here is that in pouring out ourselves we find that we take up the true life for which God has created us. As we pour ourselves out, we find that we come closer to the God who is forever pouring himself out for us. Wherever our love, our being poured out, takes us, the God who pours himself out for us is ahead of us, calling us on our way.

However, if we love, if we pour ourselves out, we need to be prepared for the negative reactions of the world to such love. Christ's life shows us the dangers of love: 'if you love enough you will be killed. Humankind inevitably rejects the only solution to its problem, the solution of love.'[9]

Contrary to our polite rejection of anger, we saw too that love is not opposed to the holy anger we encounter in God. Human anger makes us red-faced, God's anger transforms the situations with which he is angry. Where there is misery and injustice we should get angry. We encountered Carolyn Forché's lesson from El Salvador: 'You have to be able to see the world as it is, to see how it is put together, and you have to be able to say what you see. And get angry.'[10] A crucial part of holy anger is seeing the world as it really is, seeking out truth in a world of misinformation and deceit. But holy anger does not stop there. We need to cultivate a holy anger that sees the world as it is and participates in God's transformation of it. As King noted: 'It is not enough for people to be angry – the supreme task is to organize and unite people so that their anger becomes a transforming force.'[11]

To see the world as it really is requires us to acknowledge God's jealousy of all the very many idols we make for ourselves, those bits of the created order we put in the rightful place of God in our lives. To see the world as it really is means naming such idols, and cultivating the habits and practices of Christian attention and observation that will help us from the slide into idolatry. Our selfish jealousy for ourselves contrasts with God's jealousy *for* us. We can cultivate a divine jealousy of those with wisdom and maturity in the Christian life to inspire us to seek more of God in our lives, and to knock down all the very many idols we put in between ourselves and him.

Finally, we can pray. All Christian action begins and ends in prayer. Prayer itself is God's gratuitous invitation to us to participate in his work in the world, to achieve what he has decided will be achieved through prayer, and to enter into an intimate communion with him. Prayer requires awareness of ourselves, awareness of God, and most basically of all, time spent with him.

If, as Christians, we are to participate in God's action in the world in the way in which he wills and inspired by the way in which he reveals himself to be, these are the ingredients of Christian action. We acknowledge God's transcendence over his creation and our own limitations within the created order, we seek to alleviate suffering where we encounter it, to break open the cycles of misery when we uncover them, to see the world as it really is, to transform those situations of injustice with a holy anger, to name the idols that get in the way of our living the Christian life and, most of all, to pray. To begin and end all that we do and think and say with the simple offering of ourselves to God in prayer, and to trust that the simple, impassible, loving, angry, merciful, just, and jealous God who is always offering himself to us is already going ahead of us, transforming the injustices of this world and inviting us to share with him in that task of transformation. 'He is going ahead of you ... there you will see him.'[12]

Notes

1 King, *Letter from Birmingham Jail*, p. 14.

2 Cf. Gal. 6.15.

3 Moltmann, *The Crucified God*, p. 212.

4 See Cuff, S., *Love in Action*, pp. 27–51 for the recognition within Catholic Social Teaching of the inviolable dignity of each human being as a reflection on what it means to be created in the image of God.

5 McCabe, *God Matters*, p. 95.

6 Moltmann, *Crucified*, p. 326.

7 Moltmann, *Crucified*, p. 3.

8 King, *Birmingham Jail*, p. 14.

9 McCabe, *God Matters*, p. 124.

10 Forché, *What You Have Heard is True*, p. 274.

11 King, 'Honoring Mr Dubois'.

12 Mark 16.7.

Bibliography

Adamson, P. and Karfík, F., 'Proclus' Legacy', in d'Hoine, P. and Martijn, M., *All From One: A Guide to Proclus* (Oxford: Oxford University Press, 2017).

Anselm, *Proslogion* (trans. Charlesworth, M. J.) (Oxford: Clarendon Press, 1965).

Aquinas, T., *Summa Theologica* (www.newadvent.org/summa/1003. htm).

Augustine, *Homily 9* (www.newadvent.org/fathers/170209.htm).

Augustine, *On Patience* (www.newadvent.org/fathers/1315.htm).

Augustine, *Sermon 191* (www.dec25th.info/Augustine%27s%20 Sermon%20191.html).

Barrett, J. P., 'Review of 'Divine Simplicity: A Dogmatic Account. By Steven J. Duby. T & T Clark Studies in Systematic Theology, 30', in *Theological Studies* 77(4) (December 2016).

Barrett, J. P., *Divine Simplicity: A Biblical and Trinitarian Account* (Minneapolis, MN: Fortress Press, 2017).

Barth, K., *God Here and Now* (London: Routledge, 2003).

Bauckham, R., 'Only the Suffering God Can Help – Divine Passibility in Modern Theology', in *Themelios* 9.3 (April 1984).

Behr, J., 'Synchronic and Diachronic Harmony: St. Irenaeus on Divine Simplicity', in *Modern Theology* 35.3 (July 2019).

Beierwalters, W., 'Centrum tocius vite: The Significance of Proclus's *Theologia Platonis* in the Thought of Nicholas Cusanus', in *Yearbook of the Irish Philosophical Society* (2000).

Bentley, D., *That All May Be Saved: Heaven, Hell and Universal Salvation* (London: Yale University Press, 2019).

Bolton, M., *How To Resist* (London: Bloomsbury, 2018).

Bonhoeffer, D., *Ethics* (New York: Macmillan, 1950).

Bonhoeffer, D., *Letters and Papers from Prison* (London: SCM Press, 2001).

Burns, R. M., 'The Divine Simplicity' in *Religious Studies* 25.3 (Sept 1989).

BIBLIOGRAPHY

Chapman, M. D., 'The Social Doctrine of the Trinity: Some Problems', in *Anglican Theological Review* 83.2 (2001).

Cortes, E., 'Toward a Democratic Culture', in *Kettering Review* (Spring 2006).

Craig, W. L., *Time and Eternity: Exploring God's Relationship to Time* (Wheaton, IL: Crossway, 2001).

Cuff, S., 'Turning the Tables: Transforming Anger to Action', in *Crucible* (January 2019).

Cuff, S., *Love in Action: Catholic Social Teaching for Every Church* (London: SCM Press, 2019).

Cyril of Alexandria, *Second Letter to Nestorius* (www.uniontheology. org/resources/doctrine/jesus/second-letter-to-nestorius).

Cyril of Alexandria, *Third Letter to Nestorius* (www.uniontheology. org/resources/doctrine/jesus/third-letter-to-nestorius).

D'Amico, C., 'Plato and the Platonic Tradition in the Philosophy of Nicholas of Cusa', in Kim, A., *Brill's Companion to German Platonism* (Leiden: Brill, 2019).

Davies, B. (ed.), *Language, Meaning and God: Essays in Honour of Herbert McCabe OP* (London: Geoffrey Chapman, 1987).

De Villiers, P. G. R., 'Communal Discernment in the Early Church', in *Acta Theologica* 17 (2013).

Dolezal, J. E., *God Without Parts: Divine Simplicity and the Metaphysics of God's Absoluteness* (Eugene, OR: Pickwick Publications 2011).

Dolezal, J. E., *All That Is In God: Evangelical Theology and the Challenge of Classical Christian Theism* (Grand Rapids, MI: Reformation Heritage Books, 2017).

Dolezal, J. E., 'Review of Duby. S., Divine Simplicity: A Dogmatic Account. T&T Clark Studies in Systematic Theology (London: Bloomsbury T&T Clark, 2016)', in *Pro Ecclesia* XXVI.4 (2017).

Duby, S. J., *Divine Simplicity: A Dogmatic Account* (London: T&T Clark, 2016).

Durham, J. I., *Word Biblical Commentary, Vol. 3, Exodus* (Waco, TX: Word Books, 1987).

Edwards, M., *Catholicity and Heresy in the Early Church* (Farnham: Ashgate, 2009).

Emerson, M. Y., *He Descended to the Dead: An Evangelical Theology of Holy Saturday* (Downers Grove, IL: Intervarsity Press, 2019);

Faber, F., *Hymns* (London: Richardson & Son, 1862).

Farrer, A., *The Glass of Vision* (London: Dacre Press, 1948).

Farrer, A., *Finite and Infinite: A Philosophical Essay* (London: Dacre Press, 1943/New York: Seabury Press, 1979)

Forché, C., *What You Have Heard is True: A Memoir of Witness and Resistance* (New York: Penguin, 2019).

Fowl, S. E., 'What scripture does and does not say on God', in *The Church Times* (12 February 2016) (www.churchtimes.co.uk/articles/2016/12-february/features/features/scripture-and-the-doctrine-of-god).

Fowl, S. E., *Idolatry* (Waco, TX: Baylor University Press, 2019).

Fowl, S. E., 'How To Eat Until We Are Full: Idolatry and Ways To Avoid It' (Lecture given at Seattle Pacific University 22 January 2015 and St Mellitus College 4 March 2019) (www.youtube.com/watch?v=E50Ro9xrCvQ).

Ganns, G. (trans.), *The Spiritual Exercises of Saint Ignatius: A Translation and Commentary* (Chicago, IL: Loyola University Press, 1992).

Gavrilyuk, P., *The Suffering of the Impassible God* (Oxford: Oxford University Press, 2004).

Gavrilyuk, P., 'God's Impassible Suffering in the Flesh: The Promise of Paradoxical Christology', in White, T. J. and Keating, J. (eds), *Divine Impassibility and the Mystery of Human Suffering* (Grand Rapids, MI: Eerdmans, 2009).

Gersh, S., 'Nicholas of Cusa', in *Interpreting Proclus: From Antiquity to Renaissance* (Cambridge: Cambridge University Press, 2014).

Grant, D., 'Brief Discussion of the Difference between Human and Divine חמה', in *Biblica* 91.3 (2010).

Gregory of Nyssa, *Life of Moses*, trans. Malherbe, A. and Ferguson, E. (New York: Paulist Press, 1978).

Gregory of Nyssa, *Against Eunomius* 6.3 (www.ccel.org/ccel/schaff/npnf205.viii.i.viii.iii.html).

Gutiérrez, G., *The God of Life* (Maryknoll, NY: Orbis Books, 1991).

Gutiérrez, G., 'Understanding the God of Life', in Nickoloff, J. (ed.), *Gustavo Gutiérrez: Essential Writings* (London: SCM Press, 1996).

Harvey, L., *Jesus in the Trinity: A Beginner's Guide to the Theology of Robert Jenson* (London: SCM Press, 2020).

Hauerwas, S., 'How to be Caught by the Holy Spirit' (14 November 2013) (www.abc.net.au/religion/how-to-be-caught-by-the-holy-spirit/10099524).

Heidegger, M., 'Nur noch ein Gott kann uns retten' in *Der Spiegel* (30 May 1976); (trans. Richardson, W.) 'Only a God Can Save Us', in Sheehan, T. (ed.), *Heidegger: The Man* (www.ditext.com/heidegger/interview.html).

Hengel, M., *Judaism and Hellenism: Studies in Their Encounter in Palestine During the Early Hellenistic Period* (London: SCM Press, 1974).

Hinlicky, P. R., *Divine Simplicity: Christ the Crisis of Metaphysics* (Grand Rapids, MI: Baker Academic, 2016).

Holmes, S. R., 'Something Much Too Plain to Say: Towards a Defence of the Doctrine of Divine Simplicity', in *Neue Zeitschrift für Systematische Theologie und Religionsphilosophie* 43.1 (2001).

Irenaeus of Lyons, *Against Heresies* 2.13.3 (www.newadvent.org/fathers/0103213.htm).

Jenson. R., 'Ipse Pater Non Est Impassibilis' in White, T. and Keating, J. (eds), *Divine Impassibility and the Mystery of Suffering* (Cambridge: Eerdmans, 2009).

John Chrysostom, *Paschal Homily* (anglicansonline.org/special/Easter/chrysostom_easter.html).

Kilby, K., 'Perichoresis and Projection: Problems with Social Doctrines of the Trinity', in *New Blackfriars* 81 (957).

Kim, E., 'Biblical Understandings of Time', in *Time, Eternity and the Trinity: A Trinitarian Analogical Understanding of Time and Eternity* (Eugene, OR: Pickwick Publications, 2010).

King, M. L., *"Where Do We Go From Here?" Annual Report Delivered at the 11th Convention of the Southern Christian Leadership Conference, Atlanta, GA* (16 August 1967) (www.stanford.edu/group/King/publications/speeches/Where_do_we_go_from_here. html).

King, M. L., *"Honoring Mr Dubois" Carnegie Hall Tribute to Dr. W.E.B. Dubois on the 100th Anniversary of His Birth in February* (1968) (www.ushistory.org/documents/dubois.html).

King, M. L., *Letter from Birmingham Jail* (Stanford: Overbrook Press, 1968).

Lamont, J., 'Aquinas on Divine Simplicity', in *The Monist* 80.4 (October 1997).

Lester, A. D., *The Angry Christian: A Theology for Care and Counselling* (Louisville: Westminster John Knox Press, 2013).

Martin, J., *The Jesuit Guide to Almost Everything: A Spirituality for Real Life* (New York: Harper Collins, 2012).

McCabe, H., *On Aquinas* (London: Continuum, 2008).

McCabe, H., *God Matters* (London: Continuum, 2010).

Miller, C. L., 'God as *Li Non-Aliud*: Nicholas of Cusa's Unique Designation for God', in *Journal of Medieval Religious Cultures* 41.1 (2015).

Moltmann, J., *The Crucified God* (London: SCM Press, 1974).

Moltmann, J., *The Trinity and the Kingdom of God* (London: SCM Press, 1981).

Moltmann, J., *The Church in the Power of the Spirit* (Minneapolis, MN: Fortress Press, 1993).

Moltmann, J. (ed.), *How I Have Changed: Reflections on Thirty Years of Theology* (London: SCM Press, 1997).

Moltmann, J., *Experiences in Theology: Ways and Forms of Christian Theology* (London: SCM Press, 2000).

Moltmann, J., *The Future of Creation* (Minneapolis, MN: Fortress Press, 2007).

Muller, R., 'Foreword' in Dolezal, *All That Is In God: Evangelical Theology and the Challenge of Classical Christian Theism* (Grand Rapids, MI: Reformation Heritage Books 2017).

Naím, M, *The End of Power: From Boardrooms to Battlefields* (New York: Basic Books, 2013).

Nebel, M., 'Transforming Unjust Structures: A Philosophical and Theological Perspective', in *Political Theology* 12.1 (2011).

Pascal, B., *Pensées* (Baltimore: Penguin, 1966).

Paul, I., 'On the cross when Jesus died, was "the wrath of God satisfied"?' (12 August 2013) (www.psephizo.com/biblical-studies/on-the-cross-when-jesus-died-was-the-wrath-of-god-satisfied/).

Pieper, J., *Faith, Hope, Love* (San Francisco: Ignatius Press, 1997).

Pitstick, L., *Christ's Descent into Hell: John Paul II, Joseph Ratzinger, and Hans Urs von Balthasar on the Theology of Holy Saturday* (Grand Rapids, MI: Eerdmans, 2016).

Plantinga, A., *Does God Have A Nature?* (Milwaukee, WI: Marquette University Press, 1980).

Pope Benedict XVI, *Spe Salvi* 1 (30 November 2007) (w2.vatican.va/content/benedict-xvi/en/encyclicals/documents/hf_ben-xvi_enc_20071130_spe-salvi.html).

Pope Francis, *Laudato Si', On Care For Our Common Home* (w2.vatican.va/content/__francesco/en/encyclicals/documents/papa-francesco_20150524_enciclica-laudato-si.html).

Pseudo-Clement, *Recognitions*, cited in Gavrilyuk, P., 'God's Impassible Suffering in the Flesh'.

Rahner, K., *The Trinity* (trans. Donceel, J.) (New York: Crossroad, 1997).

Rieger, J., 'Theology and Mission Between Neocolonialism and Postcolonialism', in *Mission Studies* 21.2 (2004).

Rust, E., 'Time and Eternity in Biblical Thought', in *Theology Today* 10.3 (1953).

Schneiders, S. M., 'Spiritual discernment in the Dialogue of Saint Catherine of Siena', in *Horizons* 9 (1982).

Shore, J., 'Christian woman: "She's pulled the plug on her own son, whom I love and cared for. How do I deal with my anger?"' (29 March 2012) (www.patheos.com/blogs/johnshore/2012/03/shes-pulled-the-plug-her-own-son-whom-i-love-help/)

Stead, C., 'Divine Simplicity as a Problem for Orthodoxy', in Williams, R., *The Making of Orthodoxy: Essays in Honour of Henry Chadwick* (Cambridge: Cambridge University Press, 1989).

Steiner, G., *Real Presences* (Chicago: University of Chicago Press, 1989).

Surin, K., 'The Impassibility of God and the Problem of Evil', in the *Scottish Journal of Theology* 35 (1982).

Vanstone, W. H., *The Stature of Waiting* (London: Dartman, Longman & Todd, 2004).

Von Balthasar, H. U., *Dare We Hope That All Men Be Saved: With A Short Discourse on Hell* (San Francisco: Ignatius Press 1988)

Von Balthasar, H. U., 'Introduction' in *The Scandal of the Incarnation: Irenaeus Against the Heresies* (San Francisco: Ignatius Press, 1990)

Von Balthasar, H. U., *Mysterium Paschale* (San Francisco: Ignatius Press, 2000).

Ward, G., *The Politics of Discipleship: Becoming Postmaterial Citizens* (Grand Rapids, MI: Baker Academic, 2009).

Ward, K., 'The God of the Philosophers and the God of Abraham, Isaac, and Jacob', in *The Journal of Jewish Thought and Philosophy* 8 (1999).

Weinandy, T., 'Does God Suffer?', in *Ars Disputandi* 2 (2002).

Weinandy, T., 'God and Human Suffering', in White, T. J. and Keating, J. (eds), *Divine Impassibility and the Mystery of Human Suffering* (Grand Rapids, MI: Eerdmans, 2009).

White, T. J., 'Divine Simplicity and the Holy Trinity', in *International Journal of Systematic Theology* 18.1 (January 2016).

White, T. J. and Keating, J. (eds), *Divine Impassibility and the Mystery of Human Suffering* (Grand Rapids, MI: Eerdmans, 2009).

Whitehead, A. N., *Process and Reality* (New York: Free Press, 1978).

Williams, J., 'O Rex Gentium: O King of the Nations', in *The Church Times* (21 December 2018) (www.churchtimes.co.uk/articles/2018/21-december/faith/faith-features/o-rex-gentium-o-king-of-the-nations).

Williams, R., *On Christian Theology* (Oxford: Blackwell, 2000).

Williams, R., 'Pause for Thought' on the Terry Wogan Show, BBC Radio 2 (18 October 2005) (www.chpublishing.co.uk/media/74571/life-source-extras.pdf).

Williams, R., 'The Archbishop of Canterbury's Christmas message to

RT readers' (2011) (www.radiotimes.com/news/2011-12-21/the-archbishop-of-canterburys-christmas-message-to-rt-readers/).

Williams, R., *Christ the Heart of Creation* (London: Bloomsbury Continuum, 2018).

Wolterstorff, N., 'Divine Simplicity', in Tomberlin J. E. (ed.), *Philosophical Perspectives, Vol. 5, Philosophy of Religion* (1991).

Wood, W., *Analytic Theology and the Academic Study of Religion* (Oxford: Oxford University Press, 2020).

Yee, J. L., *God Suffers For Us: A Systematic Inquiry into a Concept of Divine Passibility* (The Hague: Martinus Nijhoff, 1974).

Index of Scriptural References

Index of Names

Index of Subjects